modern triangle quilts

70 Graphic Triangle Blocks

11 Bold Samplers

Rebecca Bryan

stashBOOKS.

ctpub.com

▶▶

PUBLISHER: Amy Marson

CREATIVE DIRECTOR: Gailen Runge

EDITORS: Liz Aneloski and Donna di Natale

TECHNICAL EDITORS: Alison M. Schmidt and Gailen Runge

COVER/BOOK DESIGNER: April Mostek

PRODUCTION COORDINATOR: Tim Manibusan

PRODUCTION EDITORS: Jennifer Warren and Nicole Rolandelli

ILLUSTRATORS: Aliza Shalit and Rebecca Bryan

PHOTO ASSISTANTS: Carly Jean Marin and Mai Yong Vang

PHOTOGRAPHY by Diane Pedersen, unless otherwise noted

▶▶

Published by Stash Books, an imprint of C&T Publishing, Inc., P.O. Box 1456, Lafayette, CA 94549

Library of Congress Cataloging-in-Publication Data

Names: Bryan, Rebecca, 1980- author.

Title: Modern triangle quilts : 70 graphic triangle blocks--11 bold samplers / Rebecca Bryan.

Description: Lafayette, CA : C&T Publishing, Inc., [2017]

Identifiers: LCCN 2016027870 | ISBN 9781617453137 (soft cover)

Subjects: LCSH: Patchwork quilts. | Patchwork--Patterns. | Triangle in art.

Classification: LCC TT835 .B75823 2017 | DDC 746.46--dc23

LC record available at https://lccn.loc.gov/2016027870

Printed in China

10 9 8 7 6 5 4 3 2 1

Dedication

To my family, whom I treasure more than anything—
I love you, and you are the best!

Acknowledgments

Special thanks to Robert Kaufman Fabrics for providing all the luscious, bold solid fabrics for this book.

Thanks also to the Warm Company for providing the batting for all the quilts.

Thank you to Felice Regina for piecing *Skylines* (page 51) and to Heidi Staples for piecing the mini quilts using printed fabric (page 9).

contents

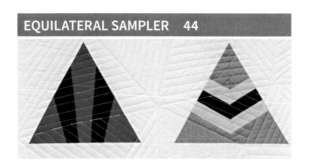
EQUILATERAL SAMPLER   44

UPSTART   47

SKYLINES   51

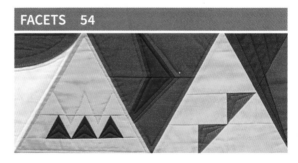
FACETS   54

right triangles 57

isosceles triangles 85

GRAPHIC RIGHT TRIANGLE SAMPLER   73

ISOSCELES SAMPLER   101

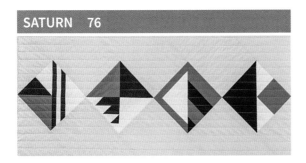

SATURN   76

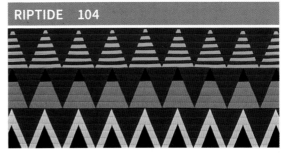

RIPTIDE   104

WAKE   79

STARDUST   107

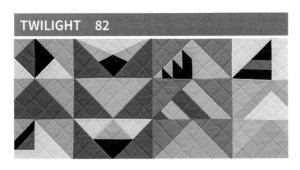

TWILIGHT   82

preface

I'm tremendously excited to share this book with you. I am not only excited about the content, but also practically giddy when I think about what you can do with that content. I hope this book inspires you to create something truly special.

Please don't feel that you have to limit yourself to using these block patterns in only these eleven quilt projects. We as quilters know just how diverse the trusty triangle can be when it comes to quilts—so the sky is the limit with these blocks. Feel free to use these blocks in triangle quilts of your own design.

I *can't wait* to see what you make!

introduction

Sampler quilts are an established tradition in the quilting world. For the uninitiated, sampler quilts are made of a mix of different block patterns as opposed to just one block pattern. Samplers are great for practicing your skills, using up scraps, or group sewing.

This book contains 70 different triangle blocks divided by triangle type. There are 36 equilateral triangle blocks, 20 right-angle triangle blocks (right triangles), and 14 isosceles triangle blocks. Choose your favorite blocks to make the sampler quilt projects. There are 4 equilateral triangle sampler quilts, 4 right triangle sampler quilts, and 3 isosceles triangle sampler quilts.

Before you get started, here are a few recommendations.

workflow

When making the triangles, you can:

• Make the triangles in batches by technique. For example, make all the triangles that use strip sets first and save all the paper-pieced triangles for last.

• Cut what you need for four blocks, make those four blocks, then cut fabric for another four blocks, and so on.

• Make each block one at a time. This way you can make deliberate design decisions about each block's appearance and how it fits within your overall concept.

special pressing note

Because of the variable nature of the quilt projects, many of the pressing instructions say to press as desired. You may find that it works better to press seams to one side rather than open. Either option is fine.

template notes

Using a trimming template is one of my favorite design techniques, especially when working with finicky angles, as with triangles. It allows freedom in making, without worrying about angles or getting the size right. It also provides precision in trimming the block to the exact size. The trimming templates are included in the pattern pullout pages.

Personally, I use both homemade plastic templates and a 60° equilateral acrylic ruler. Whatever you decide, it's important that the material you choose is clear or translucent so that you can see your design. To make my trimming templates, I simply trace the pattern onto plastic template material, which can be found in most craft stores. When I use the trimming template, I find washi tape holds the template in place while I trace the block. As an alternative you might try a sandpaper board. When I trace my block, I use a fabric marking pen or chalk. Then I use my rotary cutter and an acrylic ruler to cut along the traced lines.

a note about yardage

The yardage listed for each quilt is estimated. The yardage will vary depending on which blocks you choose, how many different fabrics you use, and how many blocks you make. I have allowed ½ yard of each color per quilt.

section introductions

Prior to delving into the blocks and the quilt projects, I have included an introduction in which I share insights specific to the triangle in that section, the color palette I chose, and the key (or index) showing each block.

elements of graphic design

Graphic design is the art of communicating content or ideas through visual mediums. I'm not a graphic designer, but I think we quilters can communicate ideas through our visual medium. This chapter briefly talks about a few elements of graphic design and how we can use these ideas in our quilts.

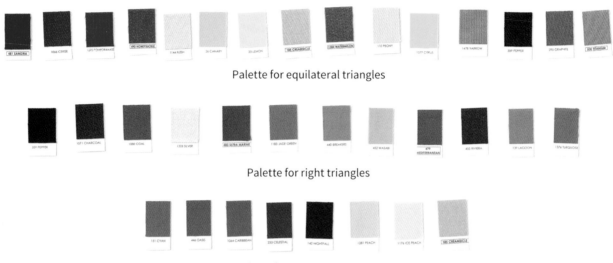

Palette for equilateral triangles

Palette for right triangles

Palette for isosceles triangles

▶▶▶

color

Color can evoke a mood. Color can be used to make something stand apart—or to minimize or hide. Color can connect or isolate. You'll see that I have used the same color palette within each section to create an element of cohesion.

Choosing colors for the quilts in this book was hugely challenging. I started by following my natural inclination to use many colors but found that result displeasing. Finally I tried using fewer colors, and I liked that better. I chose a defined color palette and then added shades and tones. When I felt the need to add color, I drew from the same palette but used a different tone or shade. The various shades added the dimension I craved.

You can see in *Riptide* (page 104) that I used various shades of peach. I don't like peach on its own, but

when I put various shades of peach together with the navy, it felt like magic.

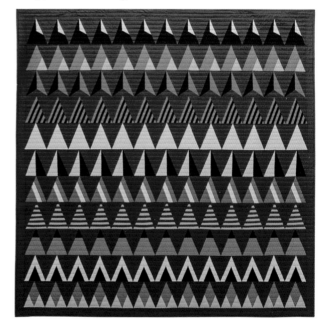

texture

Artists use texture to draw attention to the different layers of a design, to accentuate a specific feature, or to create a more visceral viewing experience. You can create texture in a quilt by using color, as described on the previous page. You can also use printed fabric. For this book, I wanted to keep my quilts uniform by using solid fabrics, but the sample blocks here show how prints give texture to the blocks.

Right Triangle Block 15, pieced and quilted by Heidi Staples

Equilateral Triangle Block 10, pieced and quilted by Heidi Staples

Isosceles Triangle Block 6, pieced and quilted by Heidi Staples

Quilting can also add texture. In *Equilateral Sampler* (page 44), I used straight-line quilting in geometric shapes. I wanted to create a texture that didn't highlight one feature but would draw the viewer deeper into the piece.

Detail from *Equilateral Sampler*

figure and ground

An object placed on a medium exists in a relationship known as the figure/ground relationship. The words on this page are the "figure," while the page itself is the "ground." In quilting, we refer to these as positive space (the figure) and negative space (the ground).

Detail of Block 5 from *Wake* (page 79)

Explore figure and ground by creating a tension between the two. This is most readily achieved through color, as shown in the examples of right triangle Block 5 (at left). The balance between figure and ground shifts just by toggling the predominant color.

In *Stardust* (page 107), I continued the triangle block design in the quilting to accentuate the negative space. Quilting in the negative space can create tension between the figure and ground.

Detail of Block 5 from *Graphic Right Triangle Sampler* (page 73)

Detail of *Stardust*

symmetry and balance

Symmetry is the familiar comfort of blocks equally distributed across the quilt top, whereas balance is the careful calibration of the weight and other visual elements of the blocks. In *Equilateral Sampler* (page 44), *Graphic Right Triangle Sampler* (page 73), and *Isosceles Sampler* (page 101), the design of the quilt is symmetrical, and the weight of the blocks is balanced within the symmetry.

Graphic Right Triangle Sampler

scale

We can play with the scale by changing block size, by giving the viewer a frame of reference, or by juxtaposing multiple sizes. In the equilateral triangle quilts (pages 44–56), I played a bit with scale. In *Upstart* (page 47), for example, larger triangles are mixed with regular-sized triangles. Scale is definitely something to explore with these block patterns.

rhythm

Rhythm may be defined as a repeating beat, or in our case, pattern. The steady rhythm of the congruent triangles allows the content of the triangles to differ. In *Facets* (page 54), for example, the facets of the diamond stand apart from the sameness, or rhythm, of the triangles.

Upstart

Facets

grid

We know the familiar block quilt grid well as a network of seen or unseen lines. But may we challenge ourselves to look beyond a common grid to surprise and engage the viewer? Grids allow structure and controlled experimentation. We can vary the scale, disrupt the rhythm, and bump up the color. We can do all this without losing the viewer, because the viewer will come back to see what happens.

Wake (page 79) uses the grid to play with many different blocks but also many variations of those different blocks. The quilt might be chaotic were it not for the grid.

pattern

Using the singular concept of a triangle, we can create elegant and complex quilt projects. Basic techniques such as constructing half-square triangles, strip piecing, and paper piecing all provide the groundwork for achieving these myriad variations on the simple triangle. We can create nearly endless patterns and variations with these triangles.

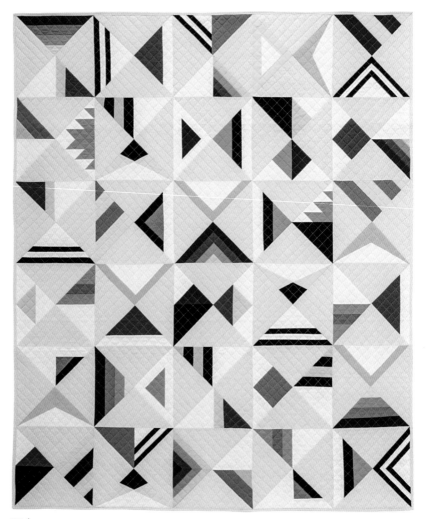

Wake

Ready? Let's begin! ▶ ▶ ▶

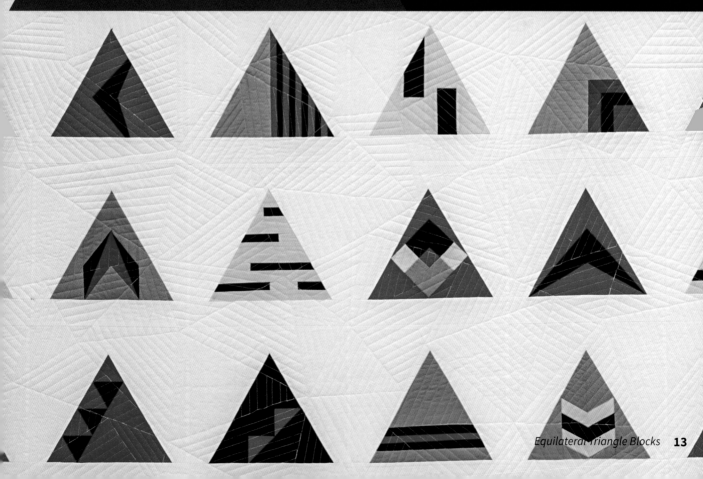

equilateral triangles

Equilateral triangles are triangles with sides of equal length and three 60° angles. I designed each equilateral triangle block to be beautiful as a stand-alone pattern and to complement the others with dramatic graphic impact.

After the instructions for making the Base block, there follow 36 block patterns. Techniques range from strip piecing, half-square triangle piecing, and paper piecing to top-stitch appliqué, and, yes, a few improvisational pieced designs. Many blocks use the equilateral triangle trimming template (pattern pullout page P4).

After the block instructions, you'll find four quilt projects. A few projects max out on triangles; a few allow you to make a big quilt by using just a small number of blocks. I'll list which blocks were used in each pattern, but please choose whichever blocks you love.

special notes

COLOR PALETTE

For this section I chose a warm color palette of purples, pinks, and yellows, with plenty of different tones to provide texture and dimension.

Equilateral color palette

TRIANGLE SIZE

It's important to note that whenever I refer to the size of the triangle, I mean the height of the triangle: most commonly 8″ finished (8½″ unfinished if you are cutting a blunt-tip triangle).

NOTE ▷ *The height of the triangle = the triangle size*

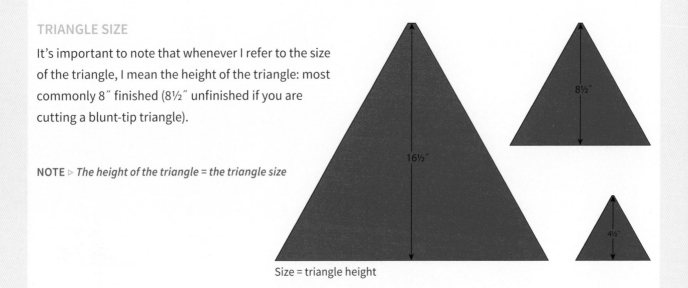

Size = triangle height

RESIZING AND SIZE OPTIONS

Nearly all of the blocks used in the quilt projects are 8″, but there are some that I sized up to a large (16″) triangle. I've provided the math for resizing each block up to a large (16″) triangle or down to a small (4″) triangle.

To make a 4″ equilateral triangle trimming template, reduce the 8″ template by 50% and redraw the ¼″ seam allowances.

To make a 16″ equilateral triangle trimming template, enlarge the 8″ template by 200% and redraw the ¼″ seam allowances.

equilateral triangle blocks

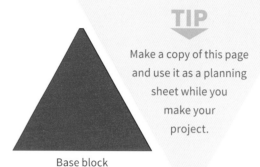

TIP
Make a copy of this page and use it as a planning sheet while you make your project.

Base block

equilateral triangle blocks (Base–Block 36)

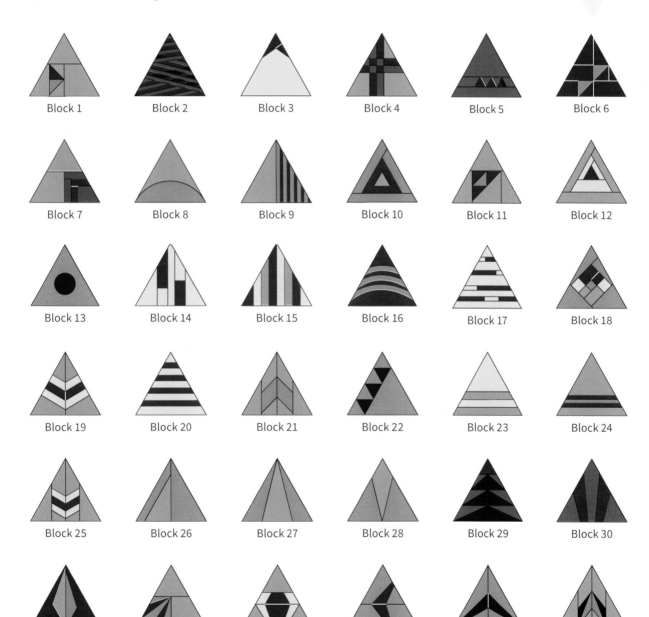

Block 1   Block 2   Block 3   Block 4   Block 5   Block 6

Block 7   Block 8   Block 9   Block 10   Block 11   Block 12

Block 13   Block 14   Block 15   Block 16   Block 17   Block 18

Block 19   Block 20   Block 21   Block 22   Block 23   Block 24

Block 25   Block 26   Block 27   Block 28   Block 29   Block 30

Block 31   Block 32   Block 33   Block 34   Block 35   Block 36

BASE BLOCK

The basic triangle for this section is the equilateral triangle. A major component of the equilateral quilts (pages 44–56), the base triangle provides a place for the eye to rest.

Cutting Several Equilateral Triangles from Yardage

To make several Base blocks, cut a strip 8½″ × the fabric width. Unfold the fabric. Using the equilateral triangle trimming template, trace the pattern pieces, and cut along the traced lines. Ideally you should be able to cut 7 equilateral triangles, assuming the usable fabric width is 40″.

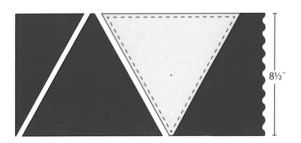

8½″

TIP You can also use a blunt-tip equilateral triangle ruler or the 60° lines on a 6″ × 24″ acrylic ruler. When using a rectangular ruler, leave a ¼″ between cuts along the raw edge of the strip for a blunt-tip triangle the correct height. Just be sure the width of the strip equals the height of the unfinished triangle. Or add an extra ¼″ to the cut size (that is, the height) and cut triangles without a blunt tip.

Cutting 1 Equilateral Triangle

Cut a rectangle 8½″ × 10″. Using the equilateral triangle trimming template (pattern pullout page P4), trace the pattern onto the fabric and cut out along the traced lines.

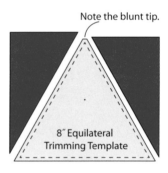

Note the blunt tip.

8″ Equilateral Trimming Template

NOTE ▷ *Whichever size triangle you are cutting, all the triangle cut sizes given are for triangles with a blunt tip on the top. Remember that the cut size given is the cut height of a blunt-tip triangle.*

Block 1

Block Stats

- Half-square triangle (HST) piecing
- Trimming template

Materials and Cutting for 8″ Equilateral Triangle

- **Pink:** 1 square 3″ × 3″, cut once diagonally*
- **Black:** 1 square 3″ × 3″, cut once diagonally*
- **Gray:** 1 square 3″ × 3″, cut once diagonally

  1 rectangle 4¾″ × 3½″

  1 rectangle 4¾″ × 6″

  1 rectangle 4½″ × 5½″
- **Trimming template:** equilateral triangle (pattern pullout page P4)

You will have 1 triangle left over.

PIECING

1. Sew the triangles together on the long sides, as shown. Press.

2. Sew the half-square triangle units together. Press the seams open.

3. Add the 4¾″-high rectangles. Press.

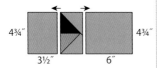

4¾″   4¾″

3½″   6″

4. Add the remaining rectangle to the top of the unit. Align the bottom left corner of the rectangle with

the half-square triangle's seam allowance. Press.

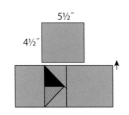

5½″

4½″

5. Trace around the equilateral triangle trimming template (pattern pullout page P4) and cut along the traced lines.

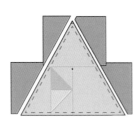

Sizing Options

	4″ equilateral triangle	16″ equilateral triangle
Pink	1 square 2″ × 2″, cut once diagonally*	1 square 5″ × 5″, cut once diagonally*
Black	1 square 2″ × 2″, cut once diagonally*	1 square 5″ × 5″, cut once diagonally*
Gray	1 square 2″ × 2″, cut once diagonally	1 square 5″ × 5″, cut once diagonally
	1 rectangle 2¾″ × 2½″	1 rectangle 8¾″ × 7½″
	1 rectangle 2¾″ × 3¼″	1 rectangle 8¾″ × 11½″
	1 rectangle 2¾″ × 3¼″	1 rectangle 9″ × 11″
Trimming template	4″ equilateral triangle	16″ equilateral triangle

You will have 1 triangle left over.

Block 2

Block Stats

- Strip piecing
- Improv
- Foundation piecing

Materials and Cutting for 8″ Equilateral Triangle

- **Muslin:** 1 equilateral 8½″ triangle*
- **Dark pink:** 2 strips 1″ × fabric width, subcut into strips 1″ × 20″
- **Black:** 2 strips 1″ × fabric width, subcut into strips 1″ × 20″

*Reminder: Equilateral triangle cut size = blunt-tip triangle height (page 14)

Note: You may need more strips, depending on your improv.

PIECING

1. Sew the strips together, alternating colors. Press the seams as desired.

2. Position the strip set, right side up, on the muslin at your desired angle, making sure the bottom corners will be covered by the strip set. Keep in mind that you will lose a ¼″ to the seam allowance on one side.

3. Flip the strip set so the right side is facing the muslin. Stitch the strip set in place along the long edge. Fold the strip set down and press.

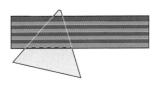

4. Using the trimming template or the muslin, trim the excess strip set from the triangle.

5. Repeat Steps 3 and 4 until the entire muslin is covered.

TIP For added seam security, consider stitching around the border of the triangle using an ⅛″ seam allowance.

BLOCK OPTIONS

This block lends itself well to creative exploration. Instead of muslin, use quilter's cotton and just cover a part of the triangle.

Sizing Options

	4″ equilateral triangle	16″ equilateral triangle
Muslin	1 equilateral 4½″ triangle	1 equilateral 16½″ triangle
Dark pink	1 strip 1″ × fabric width, subcut to 1″ × 20″	4 strips 1½″ × fabric width
Black	1 strip 1″ × fabric width, subcut to 1″ × 20″	4 strips 1½″ × fabric width

Block 3

Block Stats

- Improv

Materials and Cutting for 8″ Equilateral Triangle

- **Yellow:** 1 equilateral 8½″ triangle*
- **Black:** 2 rectangles 2½″ × 5″

Reminder: Equilateral triangle cut size = blunt-tip triangle height (page 14)

PIECING

1. Toward the top right side of the yellow triangle, position 1 black rectangle. Then flip the rectangle down so they are right sides together. Stitch along the upper edge, using a ¼″ seam allowance. Trim the yellow fabric to the ¼″ seam allowance.

2. Press the black fabric up to cover the top of the triangle.

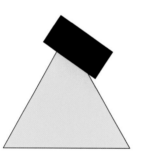

3. Repeat Steps 1 and 2 with the second black rectangle.

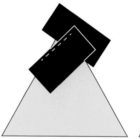

4. Trim away the excess black fabric to even up the equilateral triangle.

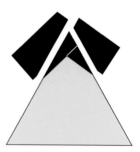

BLOCK OPTIONS

Play with the sizes of the black rectangles to alter the effect on the triangle.

Sizing Options

	4″ equilateral triangle	16″ equilateral triangle
Yellow	1 equilateral 4½″ triangle	1 equilateral 16½″ triangle
Black	2 rectangles 1½″ × 2½″	2 rectangles 5″ × 10″

Block 4

Block Stats

- Strip piecing
- Trimming template

Materials and Cutting for 8″ Equilateral Triangle

- **Pink:** 1 strip 1½″ × fabric width
- **Black:** 1 strip 1½″ × fabric width
- **Gray:** 1 rectangle 3″ × 4″

  1 rectangle 3½″ × 6″

  1 rectangle 3½″ × 4″
- **Trimming template:** equilateral triangle (pattern pullout page P4)

PIECING

1. Sew the black and pink strips together. Press the seam toward the black. Subcut 2 rectangles 4½″ × 2½″, 2 rectangles 3½″ × 2½″, and 2 rectangles 1½″ × 2½″.

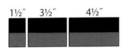

2. Sew the 2 rectangles 1½″ × 2½″ together, alternating colors. Press the seams open.

3. Lay out the block components as shown in the diagram. Then sew the pieces together into rows. Press the seams in alternating directions.

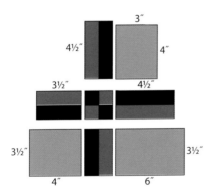

4. Trace around the equilateral triangle trimming template (pullout page P4). Leave a ¼″ seam allowance on the left side and then cut along the traced lines.

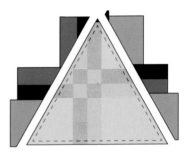

Sizing Options

	4″ equilateral triangle	16″ equilateral triangle
Pink	1 strip 1″ × 20″	1 strip 2½″ × fabric width
Black	1 strip 1″ × 20″	1 strip 2½″ × fabric width
Gray	1 rectangle 1½″ × 2″	1 rectangle 5½″ × 7½″
	1 rectangle 3″ × 2″	1 rectangle 10″ × 6½″
	1 rectangle 2¼″ × 2″	1 rectangle 7½″ × 6½″
Trimming template	4″ equilateral triangle	16″ equilateral triangle
In Step 1:	Subcut 2 rectangles 2½″ × 1½″, 2 rectangles 2″ × 1½″, and 2 rectangles 1″ × 1½″.	Subcut 2 rectangles 8″ × 4½″, 2 rectangles 6½″ × 4½″, and 2 rectangles 2½″ × 4½″.

Block 5

Block Stats

- Equilateral triangle piecing
- Trimming template

Materials and Cutting for 8″ Equilateral Triangle

- **Black:** 3 equilateral 2″ triangles*
- **Pink:** 2 equilateral 2″ triangles*

  1 strip 2″ × 10″, cut in half with a 60° angle (For printed fabrics, cut 2 strips and mirror the angles. Discard half of each strip.)

  1 strip 1½″ × 11½″; finger-press to mark the center.

  1 equilateral 6½″ triangle; finger-press to mark the vertical center.

- **Trimming template:** equilateral triangle (pattern pullout page P4)

Reminder: Equilateral triangle cut size = blunt-tip triangle height (page 14)

PIECING

1. Piece the center row together by sewing the 2″ triangles together along with the 2 pink 2″ strips. Press the seams open.

2. Add the pink strip to the bottom and the 6½″ triangle to the top. Press.

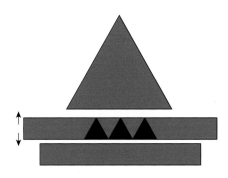

3. Trace around the equilateral triangle trimming template (pattern pullout page P4) and cut along the traced lines.

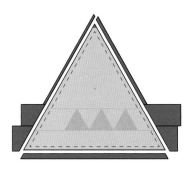

BLOCK OPTIONS

Play with the alignment of the small equilateral triangles. I chose to skew mine to the right.

Sizing Options

	4″ equilateral triangle	16″ equilateral triangle
Black	3 equilateral 1¼″ triangles	3 equilateral 3½″ triangles
Pink	2 equilateral 1¼″ triangles	2 equilateral 3½″ triangles
	1 strip 1¼″ × 5″, subcut in half with a 60° angle	1 strip 3½″ × 20″, subcut in half with a 60° angle
	1 strip 1″ × 6″; finger-press to mark the center.	1 strip 3″ × 23″; finger-press to mark the center.
	1 equilateral 4″ triangle; finger-press to mark the vertical center.	1 equilateral 12½″ triangle; finger-press to mark the vertical center.
Trimming template	4″ equilateral triangle	16″ equilateral triangle

Block 6

Block Stats

- Half-square triangle (HST) piecing
- Trimming template

Materials and Cutting for 8″ Equilateral Triangle

- **Pink:** 1 square 3″ × 3″, cut once diagonally
- **Black:** 1 square 3″ × 3″, cut once diagonally

1 rectangle 2½″ × 5″	1 rectangle 2½″ × 6″
1 rectangle 2½″ × 3″	1 equilateral 5″ triangle*
1 rectangle 2½″ × 4½″	

- **Trimming template:** equilateral triangle (pattern pullout page P4)

Reminder: Equilateral triangle cut size = blunt-tip triangle height (page 14)

PIECING

1. Sew the 3″ triangles together. Press. Trim the half-square triangle (HST) units to 2½″ × 2½″.

2. Add the black rectangles to either side of the HST units. Press.

3. Sew together into rows. The edge of the top triangle should extend roughly ¼″ past the upper right HST unit. Press as desired.

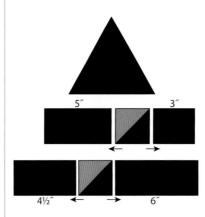

4. Trace around the equilateral triangle trimming template (pattern pullout page P4). Leave a ¼″ seam allowance for the points along the block edges. Then cut along the traced lines.

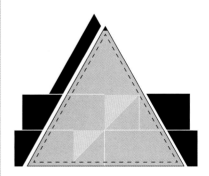

Sizing Options

	4″ equilateral triangle	16″ equilateral triangle
Pink	1 square 2″ × 2″, cut once diagonally	1 square 5″ × 5″, cut once diagonally
Black	1 square 2″ × 2″, cut once diagonally	1 square 5″ × 5″, cut once diagonally
	1 rectangle 1½″ × 2½″	1 rectangle 4½″ × 8″
	1 square 1½″ × 1½″	1 square 4½″ × 4½″
	1 rectangle 1½″ × 2½″	1 rectangle 4½″ × 6½″
	1 rectangle 1½″ × 3″	1 rectangle 4½″ × 9½″
	1 equilateral 2½″ triangle	1 equilateral 8½″ triangle
Trimming template	4″ equilateral triangle	16″ equilateral triangle
In Step 1:	Trim the half-square triangles to 1½″ × 1½″.	Trim the half-square triangles to 4½″ × 4½″.

Block 7

Block Stats

- Log Cabin–style piecing
- Trimming template

Materials and Cutting for 8″ Equilateral Triangle

- **Black:** 1 strip 1½″ × 2½″

  1 strip 1½″ × 4½″
- **Pink:** 1 rectangle 2½″ × 3½″

  1 strip 1½″ × 3½″

  1 strip 1½″ × 5½″
- **Gray:** 1 rectangle 4½″ × 6″

  1 equilateral 5″ triangle*;
  finger-press to mark the center.

- **Trimming template:**

  equilateral triangle
  (pattern pullout
  page P4)

  *Reminder: Equilateral
  triangle cut size = blunt-
  tip triangle height
  (page 14)

PIECING

1. Sew the 2½″ and then the 4½″ black strips to the pink rectangle. Press the seams open.

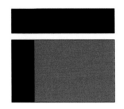

2. Add the pink strips in the same fashion. Press the seams open.

3. Add the gray rectangle and gray triangle. Press.

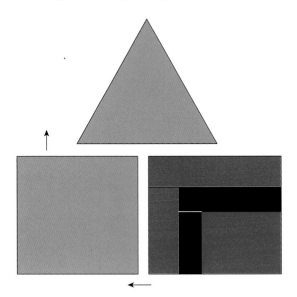

4. Center and trace the equilateral triangle trimming template (pattern pullout page P4). Cut along the traced lines.

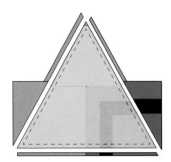

Sizing Options

	4″ equilateral triangle	16″ equilateral triangle
Black	1 strip 1″ × 1½″	1 strip 2½″ × 4½″
	1 strip 1″ × 3″	1 strip 2½″ × 8½″
Pink	1 rectangle 1½″ × 2½″	1 rectangle 4½″ × 6½″
	1 strip 1″ × 2″	1 strip 2½″ × 6½″
	1 strip 1″ × 3½″	1 strip 2½″ × 10½″
Gray	1 rectangle 2½″ × 3″	1 rectangle 8½″ × 10½″
	1 equilateral 2½″ triangle; finger-press to mark the center.	1 equilateral 9″ triangle; finger-press to mark the center.
Trimming template	4″ equilateral triangle	16″ equilateral triangle

Block 8

Block Stats

• Top-stitch appliqué

Materials and Cutting for 8″ Equilateral Triangle

• **Gray:** 1 equilateral 8½″ triangle*

• **Pink:** 2 pieces cut from the equilateral triangle
  Block 8 pattern (pullout page P2)

• **Thread:** coordinating pink for topstitching

*Reminder: Equilateral triangle cut size = blunt-tip triangle
height (page 14)*

PIECING

1. With the 2 pink pieces right sides together, stitch around the curved edge using a ¼″ seam allowance. Notch the seam allowances without cutting through the seam. Turn right side out and press well.

2. Center the pink unit on top of the gray triangle, aligning the bottom edges. Pin in place. Topstitch the pink piece in place using matching pink thread.

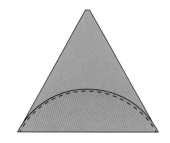

TIP Decrease bulk by trimming away the excess fabric from the curved piece. You should be able to remove a layer of gray and pink, but be sure to leave a ¼″ seam allowance on both pieces. Be careful not to trim the top layer.

BLOCK OPTIONS

To make a 4″ version, cut a 4½″ equilateral triangle. Reduce the Block 8 pattern by 50% and redraw the ¼″ seam allowances.

To make a 16″ version, cut a 16½″ equilateral triangle. Enlarge the Block 8 pattern by 200% and redraw the ¼″ seam allowances.

Block 9

Block Stats

- Strip piecing
- Trimming template

Materials and Cutting for 8″ Equilateral Triangle

- **Pink:** 2 strips 1″ × fabric width, subcut into 6 strips 1″ × 9″
- **Black:** 2 strips 1″ × fabric width, subcut into 6 strips 1″ × 9″
- **Gray:** 1 rectangle 6″ × 9″
- **Trimming template:** equilateral triangle (pattern pullout page P4)

PIECING

1. Sew the 12 black and pink strips together, alternating colors. Press.

2. Add the gray rectangle. Press.

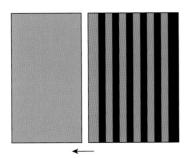

3. Center and trace the equilateral triangle trimming template (pattern pullout page P4) and cut along the traced lines.

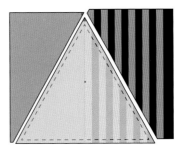

TIP Save the other half of the strip set to make another Block 9.

Sizing Options

	4″ equilateral triangle	16″ equilateral triangle
Pink	3 strips 1″ × 4½″	3 strips 1½″ × fabric width, subcut into 6 strips 1½″ × 16½″
Black	3 strips 1″ × 4½″	3 strips 1½″ × fabric width, subcut into 6 strips 1½″ × 16½″
Gray	1 rectangle 3″ × 4½″	1 rectangle 10″ × 16½″
Trimming template	4″ equilateral triangle	16″ equilateral triangle

Block 10

Block Stats

• Log Cabin–style piecing

Materials and Cutting for 8″ Equilateral Triangle

• **Gray:** 1 equilateral 3″ triangle*

• **Black:** 1 strip 1½″ × fabric width

• **Pink:** 1 strip 1½″ × fabric width

Reminder: Equilateral triangle cut size = blunt-tip triangle height (page 14)

PIECING

1. Sew the black strip to one side of the triangle. Press the seams open and trim away the excess fabric at each end, as shown.

2. Repeat Step 1 to sew the remaining black strip to the bottom and left side of the triangle.

3. Starting with the upper right side of the triangle unit, repeat Steps 1 and 2 to add the pink border.

Sizing Options

	4″ equilateral triangle	16″ equilateral triangle
Gray	1 equilateral 1½″ triangle	1 equilateral 4½″ triangle
Black	1 strip 1″ × fabric width	1 strip 2½″ × fabric width
Pink	1 strip 1″ × fabric width	2 strips 2½″ × fabric width

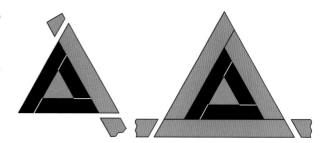

Block 11

Block Stats

- Half-square triangle (HST) piecing
- Trimming template

Materials and Cutting for 8″ Equilateral Triangle

- **Pink:** 1 square 3¼″ × 3¼″, cut once diagonally*
- **Black:** 2 squares 3¼″ × 3¼″, cut once diagonally*
- **Gray:** 1 square 5⅜″ × 5⅜″, cut once diagonally*

  2 rectangles 4″ × 5″

  1 equilateral 5″ triangle**

- **Trimming template:** equilateral triangle (pattern pullout page P4)

You will have 1 triangle left over.

**Reminder: Equilateral triangle cut size = blunt-tip triangle height (page 14)*

PIECING

1. Sew a black and pink triangle together to make an HST unit. Trim to 2¾″ × 2¾″. Add the remaining black triangles as shown. Press the seams toward the black triangles.

2. Add the gray half-square triangle to the long side. Press.

3. Add the gray 4″ × 5″ rectangles to either side. Press.

4. Finger-press to mark the vertical center of the gray equilateral triangle. Sew it, centered, on top. Press.

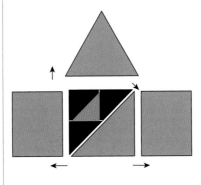

5. Trace around the equilateral triangle trimming template (pattern pullout page P4), centering the black/pink triangle. Then cut along the traced lines.

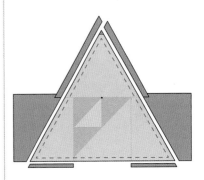

Sizing Options

	4″ equilateral triangle	16″ equilateral triangle
Pink	1 square 2″ × 2″, cut once diagonally*	1 square 5⅛″ × 5⅛″, cut once diagonally*
Black	2 squares 2″ × 2″, cut once diagonally*	2 squares 5⅛″ × 5⅛″, cut once diagonally*
Gray	1 square 3⅛″ × 3⅛″, cut once diagonally*	1 square 9⅜″ × 9⅜″, cut once diagonally*
	2 rectangles 2½″ × 3⅛″	2 rectangles 7½″ × 9″
	1 equilateral 3¼″ triangle; finger-press in half to mark the vertical center.	1 equilateral 10″ triangle; finger-press in half to mark the vertical center.
Trimming template	4″ equilateral triangle	16″ equilateral triangle

You will have 1 triangle left over.

Block 12

Block Stats

- Log Cabin–style piecing
- Trimming template

Materials and Cutting for 8″ Equilateral Triangle

- **Black:** 1 equilateral 2½″ triangle*
- **Yellow:** 2 strips 1¼″ × 6″

  1 strip 2¼″ × 8″
- **Gray:** 2 strips 1¼″ × 9″

  1 strip 2″ × 12″
- **Trimming template:** equilateral triangle (pattern pullout page P4)

Reminder: Equilateral triangle cut size = blunt-tip triangle height (page 14)

PIECING

1. To the top right and left of the black triangle, sew the 1¼″ × 6″ yellow strips. Press the seam open and trim the excess fabric after each side.

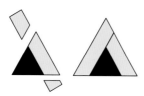

2. Add the 2¼″ × 8″ yellow strip to the bottom. Press the seam open and trim the excess fabric.

3. Repeat Steps 1 and 2 to add the gray border.

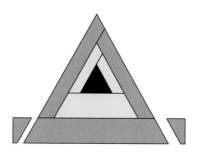

4. If necessary, use the equilateral triangle trimming template (pattern pullout page P4) to trim the block.

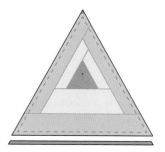

Sizing Options

	4″ equilateral triangle	16″ equilateral triangle
Black	1 equilateral 1½″ triangle	1 equilateral 4½″ triangle
Yellow	2 strips 1″ × 3″	2 strips 2″ × 8″
	1 strip 1½″ × 4½″	1 strip 4″ × 13″
Gray	2 strips 1″ × 5″	2 strips 2½″ × 15½″
	1 strip 1½″ × 6″	1 strip 3½″ × 21″
Trimming template	4″ equilateral triangle	16″ equilateral triangle

Block 13

Block Stats

- Improv
- Top-stitch appliqué

Materials and Cutting for 8″ Equilateral Triangle

- **Pink:** 1 equilateral 8½″ triangle*
- **Black:** 2 circles 3½″ in diameter, using the equilateral triangle Block 13 circle pattern (pullout page P2)
- **Thread:** matching black for topstitching

Reminder: Equilateral triangle cut size = blunt-tip triangle height (page 14)

PIECING

1. With right sides together, sew around the circles using a ¼″ seam allowance. Cut a hole in the back circle and trim the circle, leaving about ½″. Notch the seam allowance, being careful not to cut through the seam. Turn the circle right side out and press.

2. Fold the triangle in half through each side to locate the center of the equilateral triangle and finger-press.

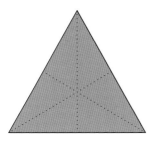

3. Place the circle over the center point of the triangle and pin or glue baste in place. Using coordinating thread, topstitch the circle in place.

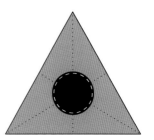

BLOCK OPTIONS

Experiment with the location of the circle within the triangle.

Sizing Options

4″ equilateral triangle	16″ equilateral triangle
Cut a 4½″ equilateral triangle. Reduce the Block 13 circle pattern by 50% and redraw the ¼″ seam allowances.	Cut a 16½″ equilateral triangle. Enlarge the Block 13 circle pattern by 200% and redraw the ¼″ seam allowances.

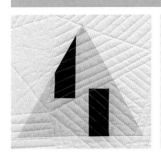

Block 14

Block Stats

- Strip piecing
- Trimming template

Materials and Cutting for 8″ Equilateral Triangle

- **Yellow:** 1 strip 1½″ × 8½″

  1 rectangle 2″ × 3″

  1 rectangle 2″ × 6″

  2 rectangles 3½″ × 5½″

- **Black:** 1 rectangle 2″ × 4″

  1 rectangle 2″ × 6″

- **Trimming template:** equilateral triangle (pattern pullout page P4)

PIECING

1. Sew together the black 2″ × 6″ and yellow 2″ × 3″ rectangles, and the black 2″ × 4″ and yellow 2″ × 6″ rectangles, at the short ends. Press the seams toward the black.

2. Lay out the pieces as shown. Sew the pieces together, aligning the bottom edges. Press as desired.

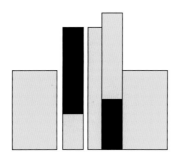

3. Trace around the equilateral triangle trimming template (pattern pullout page P4). Cut along the traced lines.

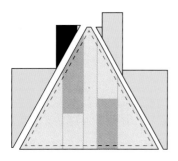

BLOCK OPTIONS

Experiment with the look of this block by flipping the layout of the 2 pieced strips. You could also lengthen the black strips to adjust the positioning up or down—just be sure to align the bottoms of the unpieced yellow rectangles.

Sizing Options

	4″ equilateral triangle	16″ equilateral triangle
Yellow	1 strip 1″ × 4½″	1 strip 2½″ × 16½″
	1 rectangle 1¼″ × 1¾″	1 rectangle 3½″ × 5½″
	1 rectangle 1¼″ × 3″	1 rectangle 3½″ × 9″
	2 rectangles 2″ × 3″	2 rectangles 7″ × 11″
Black	1 rectangle 1¼″ × 2¼″	1 rectangle 3½″ × 7½″
	1 rectangle 1¼″ × 3¼″	1 rectangle 3½″ × 11½″
Trimming template	4″ equilateral triangle	16″ equilateral triangle

Block 15

Block Stats

- Strip piecing
- Trimming template

Materials and Cutting for 8″ Equilateral Triangle

- **Gray:** 2 strips 1⅝″ × 8½″
- **Black:** 2 strips 1⅝″ × 8½″

  1 strip 2″ × 8½″
- **Yellow:** 2 strips 1⅝″ × 8½″

  1 strip 2″ × 8½″

- **Trimming template:** equilateral triangle (pattern pullout page P4)

PIECING

1. Sew the strips together, alternating the colors and using the 2 wider strips for the outer strips.

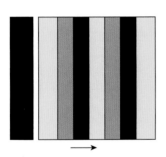

2. Center and trace the equilateral triangle trimming template (pattern pullout page P4). Cut along the traced lines.

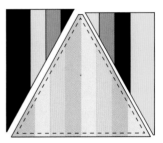

Sizing Options

	4″ equilateral triangle	16″ equilateral triangle
Gray	2 strips 1⅛″ × 4½″	2 strips 2¾″ × 16½″
Black	2 strips 1⅛″ × 4½″	2 strips 2¾″ × 16½″
	1 strip 1½″ × 4½″	1 strip 3¼″ × 16½″
Yellow	2 strips 1⅛″ × 4½″	2 strips 2¾″ × 16½″
	1 strip 1½″ × 4½″	1 strip 3¼″ × 16½″
Trimming template	4″ equilateral triangle	16″ equilateral triangle

Block 16

Block Stats

- Improv
- Top-stitch appliqué

Materials and Cutting for 8″ Equilateral Triangle

- **Black:** 1 equilateral 8½″ triangle*
- **Pink:** 3 strips 1″ × 12″, on the bias
- **Thread:** coordinating pink for topstitching
- **Optional:** ½″ bias tape maker

Reminder: Equilateral triangle cut size = blunt-tip triangle height (page 14)

PIECING

1. Make each bias strip into bias tape by folding the bias strip in half lengthwise. Unfold the bias strip and then fold and press each raw edge in to the centerline.

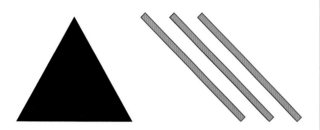

2. Position the bias tape as desired on the black triangle. To make the bias tape curve, press using steam. Pin or glue baste in place.

3. Topstitch each bias strip in place along both long edges. Trim the excess.

BLOCK OPTIONS

This block is full of possibilities. You can manipulate the bias tape in any number of ways; a loop-de-loop or flower are just two ideas.

Sizing Options

	4″ equilateral triangle	16″ equilateral triangle
Black	1 equilateral 4½″ triangle	1 equilateral 16½″ triangle
Pink	3 strips ½″ × 7″, on the bias	3 strips 2″ × 22″, on the bias
Thread	Coordinating pink for topstitching	Coordinating pink for topstitching
Optional	¼″ bias tape maker	1″ bias tape maker

Block 17

Block Stats

- Strip piecing
- Improv
- Trimming template

Materials and Cutting for 8″ Equilateral Triangle

- **Black:** 4 strips 1⅛″ × 8″
- **Yellow:** 4 strips 1⅛″ × 8″
  - 1 rectangle 2½″ × 3½″ (A)
  - 1 rectangle 1¾″ × 4½″ (B)
  - 1 rectangle 2″ × 7″ (C)
  - 1 rectangle 1⅜″ × 9″ (D)
  - 1 rectangle 1½″ × 12″ (E)
- **Trimming template:** equilateral triangle (pattern pullout page P4)

PIECING

1. First sew the 1⅛″ × 8″ black and yellow strips together into pairs. Press the seams toward the black.

2. Mark the centers of yellow rectangles A–E.

3. Lay out the yellow rectangles A–E and the black-and-yellow unit pairs as shown. Align the centers of the yellow rectangles A–E. Experiment with arrangements of the black-and-yellow pairs by shifting them left or right.

Try cutting the pairs, flipping them, and sewing them together, as in the bottom strip.

4. Sew the pieces together. Press the seams toward the yellow rectangles.

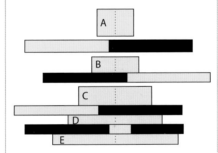

5. Trace around the equilateral triangle trimming template (pattern pullout page P4). Cut along the traced lines.

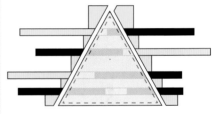

BLOCK OPTIONS

While keeping yellow rectangles A–E aligned, play with the placement of the black-and-yellow paired units.

Sizing Options

	4″ equilateral triangle	16″ equilateral triangle
Black	4 strips ⅞″ × 4″	4 strips 1¾″ × 16″
Yellow	4 strips ⅞″ × 4″	4 strips 1¾″ × 16″
	1 rectangle 1½″ × 2½″ (A)	1 rectangle 4½″ × 5″ (A)
	1 rectangle 1⅛″ × 2½″ (B)	1 rectangle 3″ × 8½″ (B)
	1 rectangle 1¼″ × 4″ (C)	1 rectangle 3½″ × 14″ (C)
	1 rectangle 1″ × 4½″ (D)	1 rectangle 2¼″ × 18″ (D)
	1 rectangle 1″ × 5″ (E)	1 rectangle 2″ × 22″ (E)
Trimming template	4″ equilateral triangle	16″ equilateral triangle

Block 18

Block Stats

- Piecing
- Trimming template

Materials and Cutting for 8″ Equilateral Triangle

- **Pink:** 1 square 1⅝″ × 1⅝″

  2 squares 5″ × 5″

  1 rectangle 2½″ × 7″

  1 rectangle 2½″ × 5″

- **Yellow:** 2 squares 2″ × 2″

- **Black:** 1 rectangle 1⅝″ × 2″

  1 rectangle 2″ × 3⅛″

- **Gray:** 1 rectangle 1⅝″ × 2″

  1 rectangle 2″ × 3⅛″

- **Trimming template:**
  equilateral triangle
  (pattern pullout page P4)

PIECING

1. Lay out the smaller pieces, as shown. Sew the pieces into rows. Press the seams in alternating directions.

2. Piece the rows together and press the seams open.

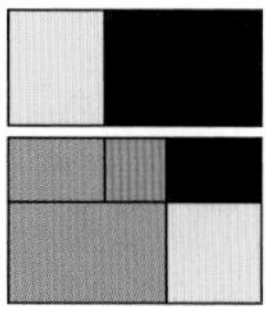

3. Sew the pink 5″ × 5″ squares on the gray sides, as shown. Add the 2½″ × 5″ pink rectangle to the right and the 2½″ × 7″ pink rectangle to the top. Press the seams toward the pink rectangles.

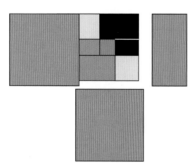

4. Trace around the equilateral triangle trimming template (pattern pullout page P4). Be sure to leave a ¼″ seam allowance along the edges of the block. Cut along the traced lines.

Sizing Options

	4″ equilateral triangle	16″ equilateral triangle
Pink	1 square 1″ × 1″	1 square 2¾″ × 2¾″
	2 squares 2¾″ × 2¾″	2 squares 9½″ × 9½″
	1 rectangle 1½″ × 3¾″	1 rectangle 4½″ × 13½″
	1 rectangle 1½″ × 2¾″	1 rectangle 4½″ × 9½″
Yellow	2 squares 1¼″ × 1¼″	2 squares 3½″ × 3½″
Black	1 rectangle 1″ × 1¼″	1 rectangle 2¾″ × 3½″
	1 rectangle 1¼″ × 1¾″	1 rectangle 3½″ × 5¾″
Gray	1 rectangle 1″ × 1¼″	1 rectangle 2¾″ × 3½″
	1 rectangle 1¼″ × 1¾″	1 rectangle 3½″ × 5¾″
Trimming template	4″ equilateral triangle	16″ equilateral triangle

Block 19

Block Stats

- Piecing
- Trimming template

Materials and Cutting for 8″ Equilateral Triangle

- **Yellow:** 4 strips 1½″ × 4½″
- **Black:** 2 strips 1½″ × 4½″
- **Gray:** 2 rectangles 4″ × 6″

  2 squares 4″ × 4″
- **Trimming template:** equilateral triangle
  (pattern pullout page P4)

PIECING

1. Sew the yellow and black strips together into 2 strip sets. Stagger the strips by roughly ½″ up for the first strip set and down for the second. Press.

2. Add a gray 4″ × 4″ square to each strip set, staggered as in Step 1. Press.

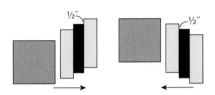

3. Add a gray 4″ × 6″ rectangle to each strip set, aligned with an end of the yellow strip. Press.

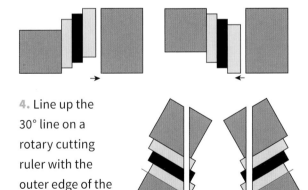

4. Line up the 30° line on a rotary cutting ruler with the outer edge of the gray rectangle in each strip set, so that all parts of the strip set extend just past the straight edge of the ruler. Cut along the edge of the ruler.

5. Sew the 2 pieces together along the cut edge. Press the seam open.

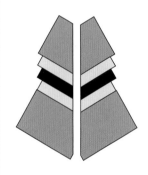

6. Center and trace the equilateral triangle trimming template (pattern pullout page P4). Cut along the traced lines.

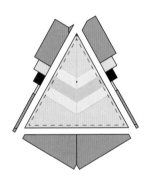

Sizing Options

	4″ equilateral triangle	16″ equilateral triangle
Yellow	4 strips 1″ × 2¼″	4 strips 2½″ × 9″
Black	2 strips 1″ × 2¼″	2 strips 2½″ × 9″
Gray	2 rectangles 2″ × 3″	2 rectangles 8″ × 12″
	2 squares 2″ × 2″	2 squares 8″ × 8″
Trimming template	4″ equilateral triangle	16″ equilateral triangle

Block 20

Block Stats

- Strip piecing
- Trimming template

Materials and Cutting for 8″ Equilateral Triangle

- **Black:** 1 strip 1¼″ × fabric width
- **Yellow:** 1 strip 1½″ × fabric width

  1 strip 1½″ × 3″
- **Trimming template:** equilateral triangle (pattern pullout page P4)

PIECING

1. Sew the black and yellow fabric-width strips together along the long edges. Press the seams toward the black.

2. From the black-and-yellow strip set, cut 1 rectangle 2¼″ × 10½″, 1 rectangle 2¼″ × 8½″, 1 rectangle 2¼″ × 6½″, and 1 rectangle 2¼″ × 4½″. Mark the centers.

3. Sew all pieces together, aligning the centers. Press the seams toward the black.

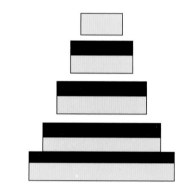

4. Trace around the equilateral triangle trimming template (pattern pullout page P4). Cut along the traced lines.

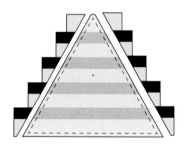

Sizing Options

	4″ equilateral triangle	16″ equilateral triangle
Black	1 strip ⅞″ × 20″	2 strips 2″ × fabric width
Yellow	1 strip 1″ × 20″	2 strips 2½″ × fabric width
	1 strip 1″ × 1½″	1 strip 2½″ × 5″
Trimming template	4″ equilateral triangle	16″ equilateral triangle
In Step 2:	From the black-and-yellow strip pair, cut 1 rectangle 1⅜″ × 5″, 1 rectangle 1⅜″ × 4½″, 1 rectangle 1⅜″ × 3½″, and 1 rectangle 1⅜″ × 2½″.	From the black-and-yellow strip pairs, cut 1 rectangle 4″ × 20″, 1 rectangle 4″ × 15½″, 1 rectangle 4″ × 11½″, and 1 rectangle 4″ × 7½″.

Block 21

Block Stats

- Piecing
- Trimming template

Materials and Cutting for 8″ Equilateral Triangle

- **Pink:** 2 strips 2½″ × 5½″
- **Gray:** 2 strips 2½″ × 8″

  1 square 2⅞″ × 2⅞″, cut once diagonally to yield 2 half-square triangles (HSTs)

  2 rectangles 3½″ × 5½″
- **Trimming template:** equilateral triangle (pattern pullout page P4)

PIECING

1. From 1 pink strip, cut 1 diamond: First make a 45° cut close to the edge of the strip. Then make a second 45° cut 2″ away to make a 2″ diamond. Cut a second 2″ diamond in the opposite direction from the remaining pink strip.

2. Make a 45° cut close to the edge of each gray strip in opposite directions as shown. Discard the small piece.

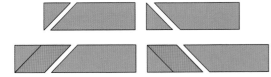

3. Sew the gray triangles, pink diamonds, and gray strips into 2 mirrored units. Press the seams in opposite directions.

4. Sew all the pieces together, aligning the bottom edges. Press as desired.

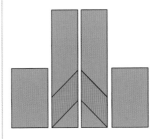

5. Center and trace the equilateral triangle trimming template (pattern pullout page P4). Leave a ¼″ seam allowance for the points along the bottom edge, and cut along the traced lines.

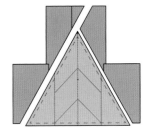

Sizing Options

	4″ equilateral triangle	16″ equilateral triangle
Pink	2 strips 1½″ × 4″	2 strips 4½″ × 12″
Gray	2 strips 1½″ × 6″	2 strips 4½″ × 20″
	1 square 1⅞″ × 1⅞″, cut once in half diagonally	1 square 4⅞″ × 4⅞″, cut once in half diagonally
	2 rectangles 2″ × 3″	2 rectangles 6″ × 10″
Trimming template	4″ equilateral triangle	16″ equilateral triangle
In Step 1:	Cut 1″ diamonds.	Cut 4″ diamonds.

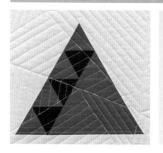

Block 22

Block Stats

• Piecing

Materials and Cutting for 8˝ Equilateral Triangle

• **Pink:** 4 equilateral 2½˝ triangles*

  1 equilateral 6½˝ triangle*

• **Black:** 3 equilateral 2½˝ triangles*

Reminder: Equilateral triangle cut size = blunt-tip triangle height (page 14)

PIECING

1. Sew the small triangles together into a strip, alternating colors. Press the seams open.

2. Add the pink 6½˝ triangle. Press.

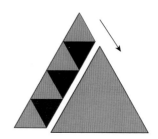

Sizing Options

	4˝ equilateral triangle	16˝ equilateral triangle
Pink	4 equilateral 1½˝ triangles	4 equilateral 4½˝ triangles
	1 equilateral 3½˝ triangle	1 equilateral 12½˝ triangle
Black	3 equilateral 1½˝ triangles	3 equilateral 4½˝ triangles

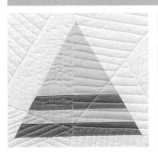

Block 23

Block Stats

- Strip piecing
- Trimming template

Materials and Cutting for 8″ Equilateral Triangle

- **Yellow:** 1 strip 1½″ × 10½″

  1 equilateral 6″ triangle*

- **Gray:** 1 strip 1½″ × 12½″

  1 strip 1½″ × 8½″

- **Trimming template:** equilateral triangle (pattern pullout page P4)

Reminder: Equilateral triangle cut size = blunt-tip triangle height (page 14)

PIECING

1. Finger-press to mark the centers. Sew the pieces together. Press the seams as desired.

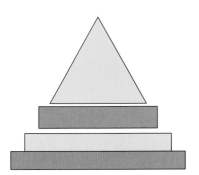

2. Trace around the equilateral triangle trimming template (pattern pullout page P4). Cut along the traced lines.

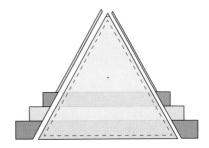

Sizing Options

	4″ equilateral triangle	16″ equilateral triangle
Yellow	1 strip 1″ × 5½″	1 strip 2½″ × 16½″
	1 equilateral 3″ triangle	1 equilateral 12″ triangle
Gray	1 gray strip 1″ × 6½″	1 gray strip 2½″ × 20½″
	1 gray strip 1″ × 4½″	1 gray strip 2½″ × 12½″
Trimming template	4″ equilateral triangle	16″ equilateral triangle

Block 24

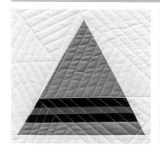

Block Stats

- Strip piecing
- Trimming template

Materials and Cutting for 8″ Equilateral Triangle

- **Black:** 2 strips 1″ × 10½″
- **Pink:** 1 strip 1″ × 10½″
- **Gray:** 1 strip 1½″ × 12½″

  1 equilateral 6½″ triangle*

- **Trimming template:** equilateral triangle (pattern pullout page P4)

Reminder: Equilateral triangle cut size = blunt-tip triangle height (page 14)

PIECING

1. Sew the black and pink strips together along the long edges. Press the seams toward the pink.

2. Add the gray strip and triangle. Press the seams toward the gray.

3. Trace around the equilateral triangle trimming template (pattern pullout page P4). Cut along the traced lines.

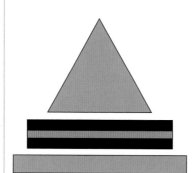

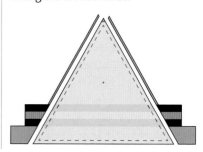

Sizing Options

	4″ equilateral triangle	16″ equilateral triangle
Black	2 strips ¾″ × 5¾″	2 strips 1½″ × 18½″
Pink	1 strip ¾″ × 5¾″	1 strip 1½″ × 18½″
Gray	1 strip 1″ × 6½″	1 strip 2″ × 20″
	1 equilateral 4″ triangle	1 equilateral 12½″ triangle
Trimming template	4″ equilateral triangle	16″ equilateral triangle

Block 25

Block Stats

- Improv
- Trimming template

Materials and Cutting for 8″ Equilateral Triangle

- **Yellow:** 4 strips 1½″ × 4½″
- **Black:** 2 strips 1½″ × 4½″
- **Gray:** 2 rectangles 2½″ × 10½″

  2 rectangles 4″ × 6″
- **Trimming template:** equilateral triangle (pattern pullout page P4)

PIECING

1. Sew the yellow and black strips into 2 strip sets. Stagger the strips by roughly ½″ up for the first strip set and down for the second. Press the seams in opposite directions.

2. Using the 60° line on your acrylic ruler, trim the strip sets to 2½″ wide.

3. Make a 60° cut in each gray 2½″ strip so that there is about 4″ on one side.

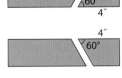

4. Add the angled gray strips to each yellow-and-black strip set. Press.

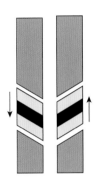

5. Sew the 2 units together. Press the seams open. Trim the bottom, leaving a ¼″ seam allowance for the point.

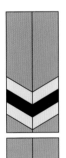

6. Add the gray rectangles on the sides. Press.

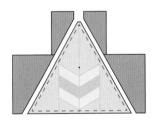

7. Center and trace the equilateral triangle trimming template (pattern pullout page P4). Cut along the traced lines.

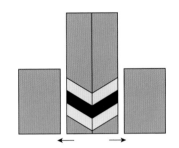

Sizing Options

	4″ equilateral triangle	16″ equilateral triangle
Yellow	4 strips 1″ × 2½″	4 strips 2½″ × 8½″
Black	2 strips 1″ × 2½″	2 strips 2½″ × 8½″
Gray	2 rectangles 1½″ × 5½″	2 rectangles 4½″ × 20½″
	2 rectangles 2¼″ × 3¼″	2 rectangles 7½″ × 11½″
Trimming template	4″ equilateral triangle	16″ equilateral triangle
In Step 2:	Trim the strip sets to 1½″ wide with the 60° line on your ruler.	Trim the strip sets to 4½″ wide with the 60° line on your ruler.

Block 26

Block Stats

- Piecing
- Trimming template

Materials and Cutting for 8″ Equilateral Triangle

- **Pink:** 1 strip 1½″ × 12″

  1 rectangle 6″ × 8½″
- **Gray:** 1 rectangle 4″ × 12″
- **Trimming template:** equilateral triangle (pattern pullout page P4)

PIECING

1. Sew the pink strip to the gray rectangle. Press.

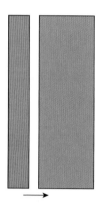

2. Line up the 30° line on your acrylic ruler with the raw edge of the pink strip, as shown. Cut.

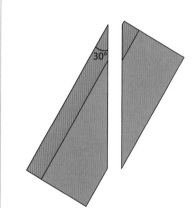

3. Add the pink rectangle to the cut edge. Press.

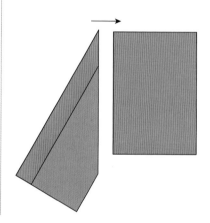

4. Trace around the equilateral triangle trimming template (pattern pullout page P4). Cut along the traced lines.

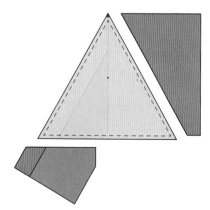

Sizing Options

	4″ equilateral triangle	**16″ equilateral triangle**
Pink	1 strip 1″ × 6¼″	1 strip 2½″ × 23½″
	1 rectangle 3¼″ × 4½″	1 rectangle 11½″ × 16½″
Gray	1 rectangle 2¼″ × 6¼″	1 rectangle 7½″ × 23½″
Trimming template	4″ equilateral triangle	16″ equilateral triangle

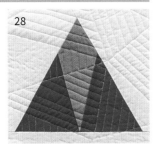

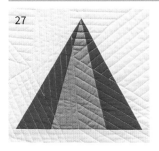

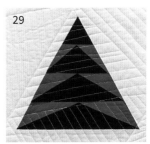

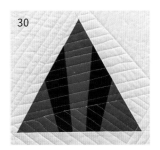

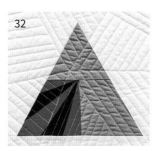

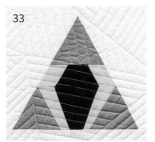

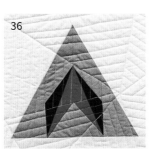

Block Stats

- Paper piecing

Materials and Cutting for 8″ Equilateral Triangle

- **Fabric scraps:** assorted
- **Pattern:** a copy of the desired equilateral triangle block foundation pattern (pullout pages P1–P4)

PIECING

1. Paper piece each block using the corresponding foundation patterns.

2. If necessary, sew the A and B foundation sections together. Press the seams open.

BLOCK OPTIONS

To make a 4″ version, reduce the foundation pattern by 50% and redraw the ¼″ seam allowances.

To make a 16″ version, enlarge the foundation pattern by 200% and redraw the ¼″ seam allowances.

equilateral sampler

Finished quilt: 72½″ × 72½″ ▲ **Finished triangle: 8″** ▲ **Finished block: 12″ × 12″**

This is the main sampler quilt for the equilateral triangle blocks, which showcases all 36 blocks. Each triangle is set into a square block. Make 1 block for a mini quilt or a pillow. Resize the quilt by increasing or decreasing the number of blocks. For a fun design idea, you could rotate a few of the blocks so that the triangles point in different directions. I added black and gray to my palette to increase the graphic impact.

Materials

Black (Kona Pepper): ½ yard

Bright pink (Kona Pomegranate): ½ yard

Medium gray (Kona Graphite): ½ yard

Pink (Kona Watermelon): ½ yard

Yellow (Kona Citrus): ½ yard

White: 5¾ yards*

Backing: 6¾ yards

Batting: 80˝ × 80˝

Binding: ⅝ yard

Cutting assumes 41˝ fabric width.

Cutting

TIP During quilt top assembly, you will be piecing the white background pieces together on the bias. It's not necessary, but you might consider starching your fabric before cutting.

WHITE

• Cut 24 strips 7˝ × fabric width. From each strip, subcut 3 rectangles 7˝ × 13½˝ for a total of 72 rectangles.

• Cut 12 strips 2½˝ × fabric width. From each strip, subcut 3 rectangles 2½˝ × 12½˝ for a total of 36 rectangles.

piecing

Use a ¼˝ seam allowance. Press seams toward the background fabric.

TRIANGLES

1. Use the equilateral block instructions (page 15) and the trimming template and foundation patterns (pullout pages P1–P4) to make the 36 equilateral triangle 8˝ blocks.

2. Trim off the lower right corner from each white background rectangle: Mark 1˝ from the corner on the long side and 1¾˝ from the corner on the short side, draw a line between the marks, and cut along the line.

NOTE ▷ *If you are using printed fabric, you will need to trim the corners from the rectangles a bit differently: 36 of the rectangles should have the lower right corner trimmed, while the other 36 should have the lower left corner trimmed.*

3. For each block, lay out 2 mirrored trimmed rectangles on the sides and 1 white 2½˝ × 12½˝ strip along the bottom of the block.

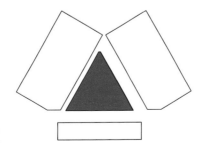

Block Stability

The 12½˝ strip will be the backbone of the resulting block. It will assist in aligning the triangles as the quilt top comes together, block by block. The strip is the only piece of the background that is not on the bias. So this piece will likely be true to size when compared with the other pieces.

4. Add the left background piece. Trim the excess fabric from the rectangle, as shown.

5. Add the right background piece.

6. Center and add the white strip.

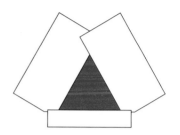

TIP Fold the white strip in half and finger-press to mark the center. You can also do this with the triangle blocks.

7. Square up the block to 12½″ × 12½″. Use the white strip at the bottom of the unit as a guide.

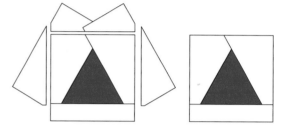

assembling the quilt top

1. Lay out the blocks on a design surface. As you evaluate your layout, think of overall color, level of contrast, and each block's piecing technique.

2. Piece the blocks into rows. Press the seams in alternating directions: Press the seams in rows 1, 3, and 5 to the right and the seams in rows 2, 4, and 6 to the left.

3. Sew the rows together. Press the seams as desired.

finishing

1. Make a quilt backing 80″ × 80″.

2. Baste and quilt as desired.

3. Bind the quilt, using your preferred method. Enjoy!

Quilt assembly

upstart

Finished quilt: 60½″ × 72½″ ▲ Finished triangles: 8″ and 16″

This playful quilt pattern is wide open to adaptation and customization. Get creative with the 36 equilateral block patterns. Play with the arrangement of triangles or copy the design as is. Experiment with pattern and color to create movement among the triangles.

The quilt I made shows 25 regular 8″ equilateral blocks and 4 large 16″ equilateral blocks. I used 11 solid-color Base blocks to add large pops of color and allow a resting place for the eye.

There are 108 possible 8″ triangles that can be pieced. As shown, there are 4 large 16″ triangles and 92 regular 8″ triangles that you could fill with blocks and color. You can also create another 16″ triangle—just take away 4 regular 8″ triangles. Likewise, you could make a few small 4″ triangles; 4 small triangles combine to make 1 regular 8″ triangle.

There's just so much you can do that I can't describe it all here. But I cannot wait to see what you come up with!

Note: For demonstration purposes, the large 16″ triangles are shown as 4 regular 8″ triangles grouped together.

Materials

Bright pink (Kona Pomegranate): ½ yard

Dark peach (Kona Creamsicle): ½ yard

Light peach (Kona Ice Peach): ½ yard

Light pink (Kona Peony): ½ yard

Magenta (Kona Sangria): ½ yard

Pink (Kona Watermelon): ½ yard

Purple (Kona Berry): ½ yard

Red-purple (Kona Cerise): ½ yard

Yellow (Kona Citrus): ½ yard

White: 2⅝ yards

Backing: 4½ yards

Batting: 68½″ × 80½″

Binding: ⅝ yard

Background Cutting

TIP Wait on this step until after you've pieced your equilateral triangle blocks. Then you will know how many background triangles you will need.

WHITE

From the white fabric, you will need to cut the background 8½″ triangles (see Equilateral Base Triangle, page 16). The number of triangles you will need depends on how many equilateral blocks you decide to make. Subtract the number of equilateral blocks made from 108 to find the total number of background triangles needed for a layout like mine.

Here's what I did:

- I cut 8 strips 8½″ × fabric width. From each strip, I used the 8″ equilateral triangle trimming template to cut 7 triangles 8½″ high. I needed 56 triangles 8½″ high.

- I cut 2 strips 9⅛″ × fabric width. From the strips I cut a total of 9 rectangles 9⅛″ × 5⅜″. I subcut each rectangle in half once diagonally to get 18 total half-equilateral triangles. (These half-equilateral triangles will go on either end of the rows.)

Here's the math so you can adapt the pattern:

For every 7 background 8″ triangles, you will need 1 strip 8½″ × fabric width.

(The number of background triangles you need ÷ 7 = the number of fabric-width strips you'll need.)

COLORED BASE TRIANGLES

From your yardage, you may consider cutting base triangles to supplement your quilt design (see Equilateral Base Triangle, page 16). I used 11 solid-color base triangles.

piecing

TRIANGLES

1. Use the equilateral block instructions (page 15) to make as many triangles as you like. I used these equilateral blocks: 1–3, 5–17, 20, 22–30, and 33–35.

2. Lay the triangle blocks and any base triangles out on a design surface. Evaluate the layout for color, contrast, and ease of assembly. Note that the quilt top will be assembled on the diagonal, which allows you to add in different-sized triangles (see Assembling the Quilt Top, below).

3. When you have chosen your final layout, add the background triangles and half-triangles to the design surface.

▶▶▶

assembling the quilt top

Assemble the quilt top by making diagonal rows. Depending on your arrangement and triangle size, use two different methods to make the rows. Sew like-sized triangles into rows (1) and different-sized triangles into groups and then double rows (2).

1. For rows with like-sized triangles, sew the rows together by first sewing the triangles into pairs. Press the seams open. Sew the pairs together to complete the row. Press the seams open.

2. For rows with different-sized triangles, you'll first need to sew the smaller triangles together into groups of 4. Press the seams open. Then piece the groups and larger triangles together into the row. Press the seams open.

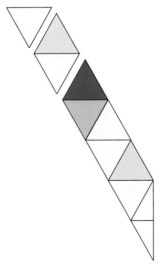

Sew triangles into rows.

Sew triangles into groups.

3. Sew the rows together to assemble the quilt top. Press the seams to one side.

finishing

1. Make a quilt backing 68½″ × 80½″.

2. Baste and quilt as desired.

3. Bind the quilt, using your preferred method. Enjoy!

Quilt assembly

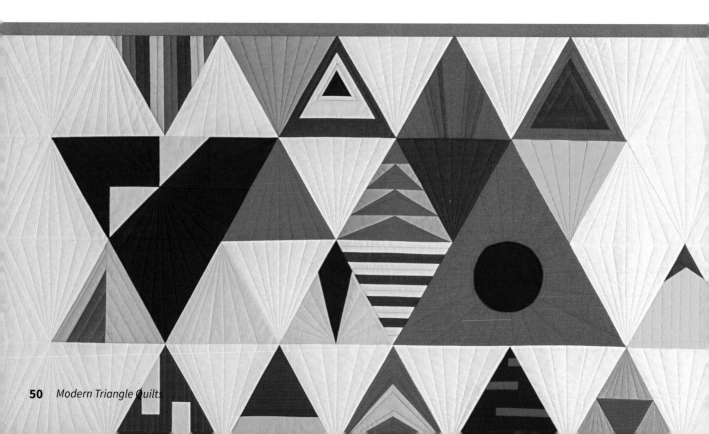

Pieced by Felice Regina

skylines

Finished quilt: 65¼″ × 80½″ ▲ Finished triangles: 8″ and 16″

The Skylines quilt allows you to make as many of the equilateral triangle blocks as you want with maximum effect, or make only a handful and still end up with a quilt large enough to cuddle. Make it your own by mixing and matching the equilateral triangle blocks to suit your preference, or copy the design as shown. Play with the pattern and color to create movement and texture.

As shown, the quilt uses 25 regular 8″ equilateral triangle blocks, 19 base triangles, and 2 large 16″ triangles.

There are a possible 44 regular 8″ triangles. Or nix the large triangles and get even more possibilities to play with a possible 52 equilateral triangles.

Size the pattern up by making the quilt wider with the addition of more triangles in the center panel. Make it long enough for a bed by lengthening the borders. If you are feeling adventurous, you could scale down the size by using 4″ triangles.

Okay! Let's get started.

Materials

Additional yardage may be needed if large 16″ triangles are pieced.

Bright pink (Kona Pomegranate): ½ yard

Dark peach (Kona Creamsicle): ½ yard

Pink (Kona Watermelon): ½ yard

Purple (Kona Berry): ½ yard

Yellow (Kona Citrus): ½ yard

Red-purple (Kona Cerise): 3½ yards

Backing: 5⅛ yards

Batting: 73″ × 88½″

Binding: ⅝ yard

Background Cutting

RED-PURPLE

- Cut 8½″ triangles (see Equilateral Base Triangle, page 16). The number of triangles you need depends on how many equilateral blocks you decide to make.

- Cut 4 rectangles 5⅜″ × 9⅛″. Cut each rectangle in half diagonally to get 8 half-equilateral triangles.

- Cut 1 piece 66″ × fabric width for the upper border.

- Cut 2 pieces 16½″ × fabric width for the lower border.

piecing

TRIANGLE BLOCKS

Use the equilateral block instructions (page 15) to make your favorite blocks for this quilt. Felice Regina, who pieced this quilt, chose Blocks 1, 3, 5–8, 10–14, 17–19, 21–26, and 29–34.

CENTER PANEL

1. Lay out the blocks, base triangles, and half-equilateral triangles on a design surface. Play with the arrangement until satisfied. The quilt panel will be assembled in diagonal rows to accommodate any large 16½″ triangles.

2. Begin assembling the center panel by first sewing the triangles into rows and groups.

To piece the rows, sew the triangles into pairs, and then sew the pairs together to complete the row. Press the seams open.

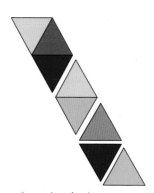

Sew triangles into rows.

For rows with different-size triangles, sew the smaller triangles together into groups of 4 and then piece the groups and larger triangles together. Press the seams open.

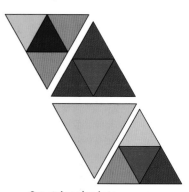

Sew triangles into groups.

3. Sew the rows together to assemble the center panel. Press the seams as desired.

assembling the quilt top

1. Piece both of the 16½˝-wide rectangles together to make the lower border, as shown in the quilt assembly diagram. Press the seam to the side.

2. Measure the center panel horizontally through the center. Trim the upper and lower borders to fit.

3. Sew the lower and upper borders to the center panel. Press the seams toward the borders.

4. Trim the upper border so the quilt top measures 80½˝ high.

finishing

1. Make a quilt backing 73˝ × 88½˝.

2. Baste and quilt as desired.

3. Bind the quilt, using your preferred method. Enjoy!

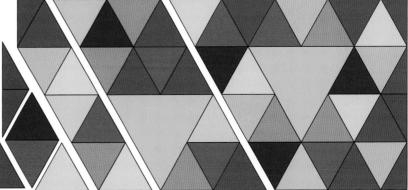

Quilt assembly

facets

Finished quilt: 30½″ × 40½″ ▲ Finished triangle: 8″

Facets is a small quilt, offering you a chance to make a project without committing to making all the triangles. You can choose up to fourteen blocks to make.

This quilt is different in that the triangles come together to form a gem shape, so consider how the blocks at the edges will define the gem shape. Play with the colors in the background to create additional movement. I personally think an ombré effect would be cool.

Materials

Bright pink (Kona Pomegranate): ½ yard

Dark peach (Kona Creamsicle): ½ yard

Gold (Kona Yarrow): ½ yard

Pink (Kona Watermelon): ½ yard

Red-purple (Kona Cerise): ½ yard

Yellow (Kona Citrus): ½ yard

Purple (Kona Berry): 1¼ yards

Backing: 1⅜ yards

Batting: 38½″ × 48½″

Binding: ⅜ yard

Background Cutting

PURPLE

- Cut 2 rectangles 4½″ × 30½″.

- Cut 1 strip 8½″ × fabric width. Subcut into 2 rectangles 8½″ × 17″.

- Cut 2 strips 8½″ × fabric width. Subcut into 2 rectangles 8½″ × 12″ and 4 rectangles 8½″ × 8″.

For the 8½″ purple rectangles, you will need to make a 60° cut at the very edge of the rectangle, as shown. Note that if you are using a printed fabric, you will need to make the cut in the opposite direction for half the rectangles.

piecing

TRIANGLES

Use the equilateral block instructions (page 15) to make 14 of your favorite 8″ blocks for this quilt. I chose Blocks 1, 5–8, 10, 12, 14, 20, 21, 29, 31, and 34. I also threw in 1 base triangle.

assembling the quilt top

1. Lay out your triangles and play with the arrangement. Note how the blocks fit together in terms of color and contrast. Also lay out the background rectangles. Can you see the gem shape?

2. Sew the triangle blocks into pairs and then sew the pairs together. Refer to the quilt assembly diagram to sew the triangle strips and background pieces together into rows. Press the seams in alternating directions.

3. Sew the rows together, along with the top and bottom 4½″ × 30½″ border strips.

TIP Fold the 4½″ × 30½″ rectangles in half lengthwise and finger-press to mark the center.

4. Trim the sides even with the top and bottom borders to square the quilt top.

Quilt assembly

finishing

1. Trim the quilt backing to 38½″ × 48½″.

2. Baste and quilt as desired.

3. Bind the quilt, using your preferred method. Enjoy!

right triangles

This section is devoted to right triangles, which are triangles with a 90° angle. These triangles are very easy to use as classic half-square triangles (HSTs). In fact, I designed the blocks to be used easily in HST patterns. So feel free to use the twenty blocks in your own HST quilt designs.

Following the instructions on how to make the Base blocks, there are twenty block patterns. Techniques involved are, for the most part, using the trimming template, HST piecing, and paper piecing.

There are four right triangle quilt projects included in this book; most make a throw-sized quilt. There are projects that max out on triangles, allowing you to experiment with block options (and there are a lot of options for this section!). There are also projects for larger quilts that use a smaller number of blocks. I'll list which blocks I used in each pattern, but please choose whichever blocks you love.

special notes

COLOR PALETTE

For this section I chose icy blues with a spicy yellow and soothing teals. If I want a sharp and graphic look, I use fewer colors, but when I want more texture, I use more shades and tones.

359 PEPPER   1071 CHARCOAL   1080 COAL   1333 SILVER   483 ULTRA MARINE   1183 JADE GREEN

440 BREAKERS   452 WASABI   479 MEDITERRANEAN   455 RIVIERA   139 LAGOON   1376 TURQUOISE

Right triangle color palette

TRIANGLE SIZE

All triangles in this section are the same size. Each triangle measures 8″ finished on the short sides and can be used in any quilt design for 8″ finished blocks.

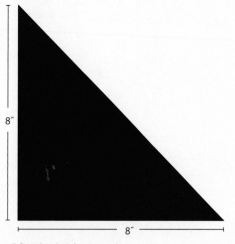

8″ finished right triangle

BLOCK OPTIONS

The possibilities for creating derivatives of these block patterns are nearly endless. Just within the twenty block patterns I provide, there are many options. I'll show you when we get to each block, so be on the lookout for block options.

right triangle blocks

right triangle blocks (Base–Block 20)

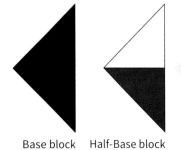

Base block   Half-Base block

TIP

Make a copy of this page and use it as a planning sheet while you make your project.

Block 1   Block 2   Block 3   Block 4   Block 5

Block 6   Block 7   Block 8   Block 9   Block 10

Block 11   Block 12   Block 13   Block 14   Block 15

Block 16   Block 17   Block 18   Block 19   Block 20

BASE BLOCK

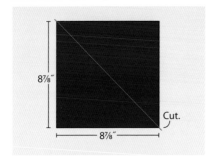

Let's start with the basics! These are the two basic right triangles that are the easiest to make. These base blocks do a couple of things. One, the base triangles give the eye a place to rest in an otherwise busy quilt. And two, when you are *done* with a quilt but the quilt isn't, throw in some base triangles to finish it up!

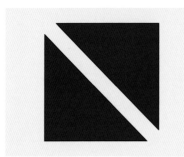

To make the Base block, cut a square $8\frac{7}{8}'' \times 8\frac{7}{8}''$ and then cut the square in half once diagonally. This yields 2 Base blocks.

HALF-BASE BLOCK

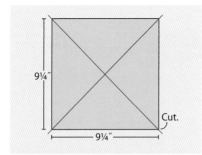

A Half-Base block is just that: half of a Base block. To make a Half-Base block, cut a square $9\frac{1}{4}'' \times 9\frac{1}{4}''$ and then cut the square in half twice diagonally. This will yield 4 quarter-square triangles for 4 Half-Base blocks.

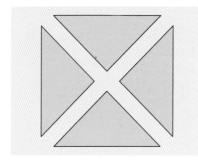

TIPS

• Sew 2 Half-Base blocks together and you've got a swell-looking block.

• Cut a group of Half-Base blocks before piecing the blocks for your selected quilt project. This way you'll have Half-Base blocks at the ready to make Halfsie blocks.

Make Halfsie blocks from a pieced triangle and a Half-Base block.

Halfsie block

Block 1

Block Stats

- Trimming template
- Lots of block options

Materials and Cutting for 8″ Right Triangle

- **Blue:** 2 strips 2½″ × 10″
- **Black:** 2 strips 2½″ × 10″
- **Trimming template:** right triangle (pattern pullout page P4)

PIECING

1. Sew the strips together, alternating colors. Press to one side.

2. Trace around the right triangle trimming template (pattern pullout page P4). Cut along the traced lines.

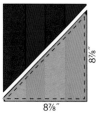

BLOCK OPTIONS

By using the half-base trimming template (pattern pullout page P3), you can cut half-base units from the strip set in interesting ways. And—oh, look—there's a smaller version of Block 19!

And by using different colors or by rotating the direction of the trimming template, you will find different looks.

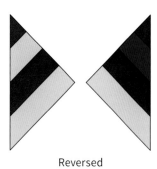

Reversed

Block 2

Block Stats

• Strip piecing

• Trimming template

Materials and Cutting for 8″ Right Triangle

• **White:** 1 rectangle 4½″ × 13″

  1 strip 1¼″ × 13″

• **Black:** 2 strips 1¼″ × 13″

• **Trimming template:** right triangle
  (pattern pullout page P4)

PIECING

1. Piece the white and black strips together. Press the seams to one side.

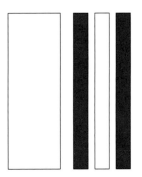

2. Position the right triangle trimming template (pattern pullout page P4) so that the long side of the triangle aligns with the edge of black fabric. Trace around the template and cut along the traced lines.

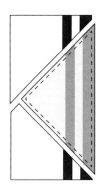

BLOCK OPTIONS

Flip the orientation of the trimming template for a different look.

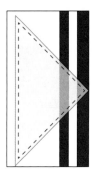

Block 3

Block Stats

- Half-square triangle (HST) piecing

Materials and Cutting for 8″ Right Triangle

- **White:** 2 squares 4⅞″ × 4⅞″, cut once diagonally*

- **Blue:** 1 square 4⅞″ × 4⅞″, cut once diagonally*

There will be 1 extra triangle.

PIECING

1. Sew 1 white triangle and 1 blue triangle together on the long sides. Press the seam to one side.

2. Add 1 white triangle to the blue side. Press the seam toward the white triangle.

3. Add the remaining white triangle. Press the seam toward the white triangle.

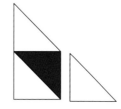

BLOCK OPTIONS

Add a third color and rotate the half-square triangle to make this block variation.

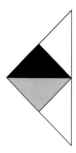

Block 4

Block Stats

• Strip piecing

• Half-base trimming template

Materials and Cutting for 8″ Right Triangle

• **Black:** 4 strips 1½″ × 10″

• **Yellow:** 4 strips 1½″ × 10″

• **Trimming template:** half-base (pullout page P3)

PIECING

1. Make 2 strip sets. Press the seams in one direction for one set and in the opposite direction for the other.

Make 2.

2. Align the half-base trimming template (pattern pullout page P3) with the yellow side of a strip set. Trace the template and cut along the traced lines. Repeat for the second strip set.

3. Sew the 2 pieced triangles together along the short sides. Press the seam open.

BLOCK OPTIONS

In Step 2, rotate the orientation of the trimming template.

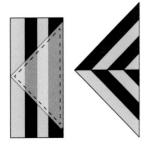

HALFSIES

Make Halfsie blocks by piecing each half to a Half-Base block (page 60).

Block 5

Block Stats

- Log Cabin–style piecing
- Trimming template

Materials and Cutting for 8″ Right Triangle

- **Blue:** 1 square 4⅞″ × 4⅞″, cut once diagonally*
- **White:** 1 strip 2″ × fabric width. Cut into rectangles 2″ × 8″, 2″ × 10″, and 2″ × 16″.
- **Trimming template:** right triangle (pattern pullout page P4)

You will have 1 extra triangle.

PIECING

1. Sew the white 2″ × 8″ rectangle to one short side of the blue triangle. Press the seam open.

2. Add the white 2″ × 10″ rectangle to the opposite side. Press the seam open.

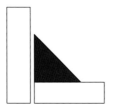

3. Trim the white ends that extend past the edge of the triangle.

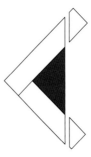

4. Add the 2″ × 16″ rectangle, centered. Press the seam open.

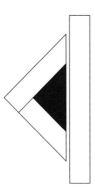

5. Center and trace around the right triangle trimming template (pattern pullout page P4). Cut along the traced lines.

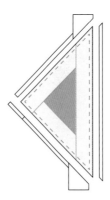

Block 6

Block Stats

• Half-square triangle (HST) piecing

Materials and Cutting for 8″ Right Triangle

• **Black:** 1 Half-Base block (page 60)

• **Blue:** 1 square 4⅞″ × 4⅞″, cut once diagonally*

• **White:** 1 square 4⅞″ × 4⅞″, cut once diagonally*

There will be 1 extra triangle.

PIECING

1. Sew the blue and white triangles together, as shown. Press the seam open.

2. Sew the pieced triangle to the Half-Base block (page 60). Press the seams toward the Half-Base block.

BLOCK OPTIONS

Change up the color placement of the HSTs to alter the look.

Block 7

Block Stats

- Strip piecing
- Half-base trimming template

Materials and Cutting for 8″ Right Triangle

- **Yellow:** 2 strips 1½″ × 10″
- **White:** 2 rectangles 3⅝″ × 10″
- **Trimming template:** half-base (pattern pullout page P3)

PIECING

1. Sew a yellow strip to each white rectangle. Press in opposite directions.

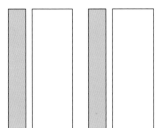

2. For each unit, align the long side of the half-base trimming template (pattern pullout page P3) with the edge of the yellow fabric. Trace around the template and cut along the traced lines.

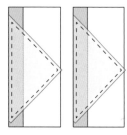

3. Sew the halves together, as shown. Press the seam open.

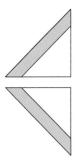

BLOCK OPTIONS

After Step 2, sew each half to a Half-Base block (page 60). Press.

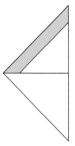

Block 8

Block Stats

- Piecing
- Block options

Materials and Cutting for 8″ Right Triangle

- **White:** 1 and 1 reversed using right triangle Block 8 template A (pullout page P1)

  1 and 1 reversed using right triangle Block 8 template B (pullout page P1)

  1 square 3¼″ × 3¼″, cut twice diagonally to yield 4 triangles (C); you will have 2 extra.
- **Blue:** 3 squares 2⅞″ × 2⅞″, cut once diagonally (D)

  1 square 3¼″ × 3¼″, cut twice diagonally to yield 4 triangles (E); you will have 2 extra.
- **Optional:** right triangle trimming template (pattern pullout page P4)

PIECING

1. Lay the pieces out as shown.

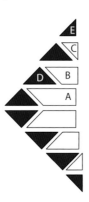

2. Sew the pieces together to make a row. Press the seams open. It may help to mark the intersections of the ¼″ seam allowances for accurate piecing.

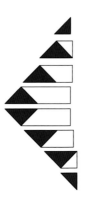

3. Sew the rows together. Press the seams as desired.

4. If needed, position the right triangle trimming template (pattern pullout page P4) so that the triangle points align with the ¼″ seamline. Trace around the template and cut along the traced lines.

BLOCK OPTIONS

Instead of piecing the halves together, piece each half to a Half-Base block (page 60). Press.

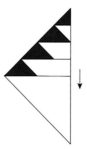

Block 9

Block Stats

- Half-square triangle (HST) piecing

Materials and Cutting for 8″ Right Triangle

- **Blue:** 1 square 4½″ × 4½″
- **White:** 1 square 4⅞″ × 4⅞″, cut diagonally once

PIECING

1. Sew a white triangle to the top of the blue square. Press the seam toward the triangle.

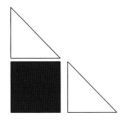

2. Sew the second triangle to the right of the blue square. Press the seam toward the triangle.

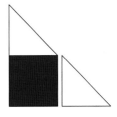

Block 10

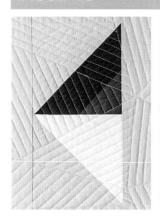

Block Stats

- Strip piecing
- Half-base trimming template

Materials and Cutting for 8″ Right Triangle

- **Blue:** 1 strip 2⅝″ × 10″
- **Black:** 1 strip 2½″ × 10″
- **White:** 1 Half-Base block (page 60)
- **Trimming template:** half-base (pattern pullout page P3)

PIECING

1. Sew the blue and black strips together. Press the seam toward the black strip.

2. Trace around the half-base trimming template (pattern pullout page P3). Cut along the traced lines.

3. Add the Half-Base block. Press the seam toward the Half-Base block.

BLOCK OPTIONS

Instead of sewing the unit to a Half-Base block, double it up and sew the 2 units together.

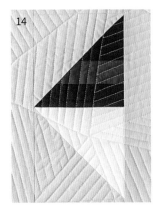

Materials and Cutting for 8″ Right Triangle

- **Fabric scraps:** assorted

- **Pattern:** a copy of the desired right triangle block
  foundation pattern (pullout pages P1 and P4)

PIECING

1. Paper piece each block using the corresponding foundation patterns.

Note:

For Block 11, make 2 foundations and sew them together along the short sides.

For Blocks 13, 14, 15, and 17, sew the foundation-pieced half-base unit to a Half-Base block.

For Blocks 12 and 16, sew foundations A and B together. Press the seams open.

Sew paper-pieced triangles together (Block 11 shown).

BLOCK OPTIONS

Repeat Step 1 above to make a second pieced unit. Rotate one of the units to make this variation.

Block 17 variation

REFLECTION

Instead of sewing the unit to a Half-Base block (page 60), sew the pieced unit you made in Step 1 to a mirrored version. You'll need to make a mirrored version of the template and then paper piece it as directed in Step 1. Sew the pieces together and press the seam open.

Block 17 variation

HALFSIES

Instead of piecing the halves together, sew the halves to a Half-Base block (page 60). Press the seams toward the Half-Base block.

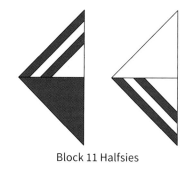

Block 11 Halfsies

graphic right triangle sampler

Finished quilt: 62″ × 70½″ ▲ Finished triangle: 8″

Try your hand at making all twenty right triangle blocks (plus one extra) in this graphic and bold sampler quilt. Keep the palette simple and elegant by choosing just a few colors, or spice it up by adding more.

As shown, the quilt finishes at a nice throw size, but you could beef up the borders for a bed quilt or scale down the size of the triangles for a smaller version.

Materials

Black (Kona Pepper): ½ yard

Blue (Kona Riviera): ½ yard

White (Kona Snow): ½ yard

Yellow-green (Kona Wasabi): ½ yard

Light gray (Kona Ash):
4 yards for background

Backing: 4⅝ yards

Batting: 70″ × 80½″

Binding: ⅝ yard of light gray
(Kona Ash)

Cutting

LIGHT GRAY

- Cut 3 strips 9¼″ × fabric width.
  Subcut into 11 squares 9¼″ × 9¼″.

  Subcut each square diagonally twice
  to yield 44 quarter-square triangles
  (2 will be extra).

- Cut 2 strips 6¼″ × fabric width.
  Subcut into 14 pieces 6¼″ × 4½″ (A).

- Cut 6 strips 6¼″ × fabric width.

  Subcut 4 strips into 4 pieces
  6¼″ × 22½″ (D) and 4 pieces
  6¼″ × 15½″ (C). Subcut the other
  2 strips into 2 pieces 6¼″ × 15½″ (C)
  and 4 pieces 6¼″ × 8½″ (B).

- Cut 12 strips 2½″ × fabric width. Trim
  each strip to 2½″ × 36¾″.

- Cut 4 strips 5½″ × fabric width. Trim
  each strip to 5½″ × 36¾″.

piecing

1. Use the right triangle block instructions (page 59) to make 1 of each block, plus 1 extra of your choosing. (I made an extra Block 6.) Make a total of 21 right triangle blocks.

2. Sew a background triangle to the left side of each right triangle block. Press the seams toward the background.

3. Sew a second background triangle to the right side of each right triangle block. Press the seams toward the background. Trim off the dog-ears.

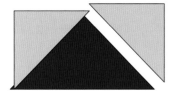 

4. Lay out the block units and background pieces A–D, using the quilt assembly diagram as a guide.

5. Sew the blocks into columns with the A, B, C, and D pieces. Press the seams away from the blocks.

TIP Before piecing the rows, mark the centers of the A pieces along the 4½″ sides. This will help to align the rows during the last step.

6. Sew the 12 strips 2½″ × 36¾″ in pairs to make 6 sashing strips. Press the seams to one side.

7. Sew the 4 strips 5½″ × 36¾″ in pairs to make 2 borders. Press the seams to one side.

8. Lay out the columns, sashing, and border strips. Sew together to assemble the quilt top. Press the seams toward the sashing strips.

TIP As you sew the rows together, align the point of each right triangle block with the center mark of the adjacent A piece.

9. Trim the top and bottom to square up the quilt top.

finishing

1. Make a quilt backing 70″ × 80″.

2. Baste and quilt as desired.

3. Bind the quilt, using your preferred method. Enjoy!

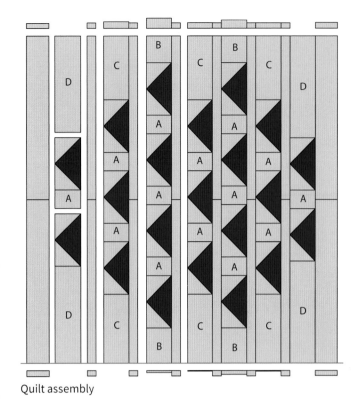

Quilt assembly

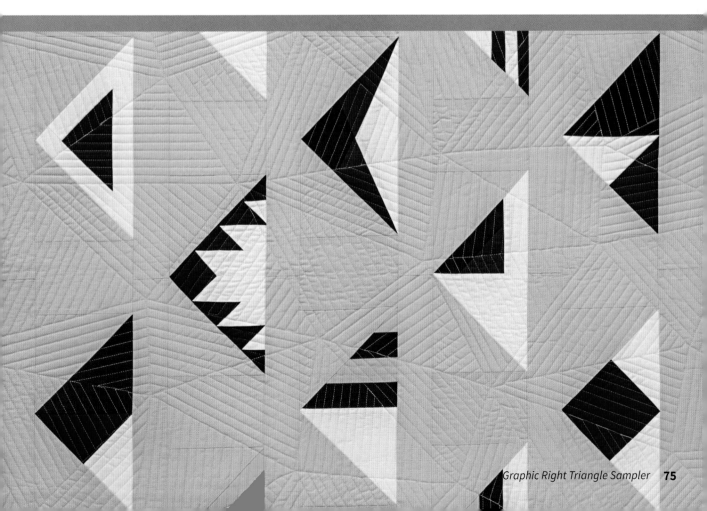

saturn

Finished quilt: 62¾″ × 62¾″ ▲ Finished triangle: 8″

Saturn features up to 32 right triangle blocks. Make any combination of your favorite right triangle blocks, or consider mixing in some Base blocks (page 60). I chose to make 25 right triangle blocks and 1 Half-Base block; I substituted base triangles for the rest.

As shown, the triangles finish at 8″. Adapt the finished size of the quilt by adding borders, or scale the blocks down to 4″ or 6″.

Materials

Blue-green (Kona Jade Green): ½ yard

Deep gray (Kona Charcoal): ½ yard

White (Kona Snow): ½ yard

Pale gray (Kona Silver): 3¾ yards*

Backing: 4⅛ yards

Batting: 70¾″ × 70¾″

Binding: ⅝ yard

*Requires at least 40½″ of usable fabric width or additional yardage to piece.

Cutting

PALE GRAY

• Cut 15 strips 8½″ × fabric width.

From 6 strips, subcut 12 rectangles 8½″ × 16½″ (A).

From 3 strips, subcut 10 squares 8½″ × 8½″ (B).

From 1 strip, subcut 2 rectangles 8½″ × 20½″ (C).

From 5 strips, subcut 5 rectangles 8½″ × 40½″ (D).

piecing

TRIANGLE PAIRS

1. Use the right triangle block instructions (page 59) to make 32 right triangle blocks. I used Blocks 1–9 and 11–18.

2. Refer to the quilt assembly diagram (page 78) to experiment with the block layout. Think about color and balance.

3. Piece the right triangle blocks into pairs. Press the seams as desired. Make 16 pairs.

ASSEMBLING THE QUILT TOP

1. Referring to the quilt assembly diagram, lay out the triangle pairs and pieces A–D.

2. Sew the triangle pairs and rectangles A, B, C, and D into diagonal rows. Press the seams open.

TIP While you are piecing the units into rows, take care that the orientation of the triangle pairs remains as planned.

3. Sew the rows together, aligning and pinning the corners of the triangle pairs first. Press the seams as desired.

TIP Work from the center row out, matching and pinning the triangle units first. This will help ensure proper placement and spacing of the triangle units.

4. Square up the quilt top. Leave a ¼″ seam allowance where the points meet the quilt edge.

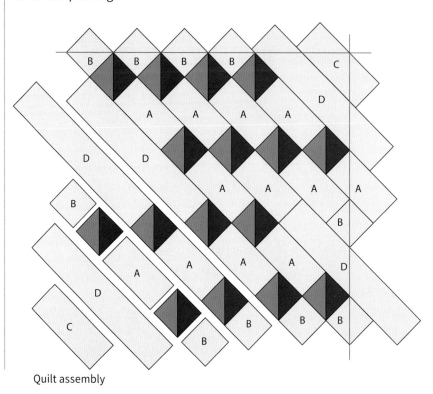

Quilt assembly

finishing

1. Make a quilt backing 70¾″ × 70¾″.

2. Baste and quilt as desired.

3. Bind the quilt, using your preferred method. Enjoy!

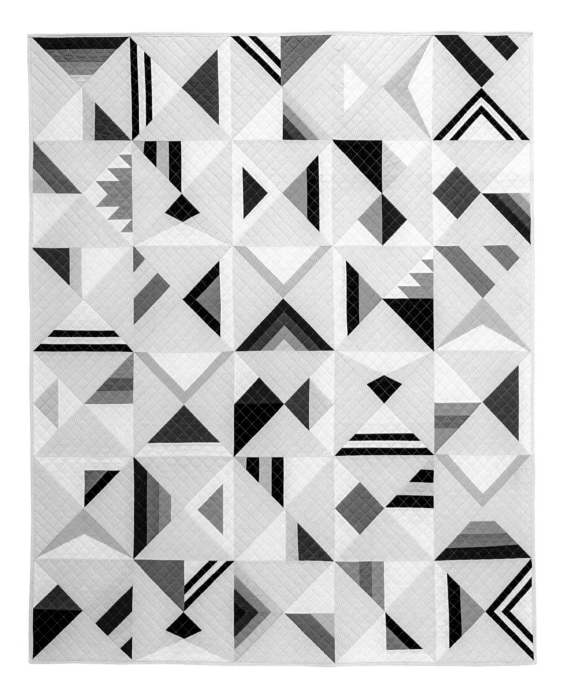

wake

Finished quilt: $57\frac{3}{8}'' \times 68\frac{3}{4}''$ ▲ Finished triangle: $8''$ ▲ Finished block: $11\frac{3}{8}'' \times 11\frac{3}{8}''$

Wake allows you plenty of opportunity to play. In this quilt, the right triangle blocks are sewn in combination into different square blocks. This quilt uses three of each block. Instead of making three of the exact same block, keep the viewer guessing by changing up the look of the block using the block options, color, or halfsie options.

Materials

Aqua (Kona Breakers): ½ yard

Black (Kona Pepper): ½ yard

Dark teal (Kona Celestial): ½ yard

Light green (Kona Pond): ½ yard

Teal (Kona Ultra Marine): ½ yard

Turquoise (Kona Turquoise): ½ yard

Yellow-green (Kona Wasabi): ½ yard

Pale gray (Kona Silver): 2¼ yards

Backing: 3¾ yards

Batting: 65½″ × 77″

Binding: ⅝ yard

Background Cutting

PALE GRAY

- Cut 8 strips 8⅞″ × fabric width. Subcut into 30 squares 8⅞″ × 8⅞″.

  Subcut each square diagonally once to yield 2 triangles for a total of 60 background triangles.

piecing

1. Use the right triangle block instructions (page 59) to make 60 right triangle blocks. I chose to make 3 of each block, but you may choose differently.

2. Piece each triangle block to a background triangle along the short sides. Press.

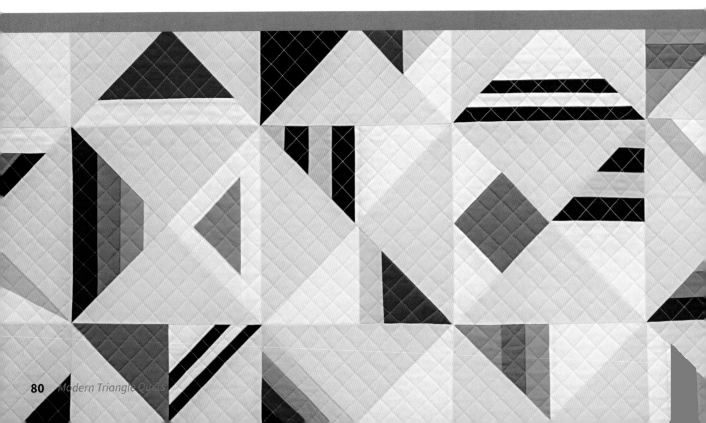

assembling the quilt top

1. Lay the pieced triangles out on a design surface and play with the arrangement. While you finalize your design, think about balance in color and contrast, block type, and ease of assembly.

2. Sew the triangle pieces together to form square blocks. Press the seams open. Each square block should measure 11⅞″ × 11⅞″ unfinished.

3. Piece the squares into columns. Press the seams in alternating directions: For columns 1, 3, and 5, press the seams up. For rows 2 and 4, press the seams down.

4. Sew the columns together. Press the seams as desired.

Quilt assembly

finishing

1. Make a quilt backing 65½″ × 77″.

2. Baste and quilt as desired.

3. Bind the quilt, using your preferred method. Enjoy!

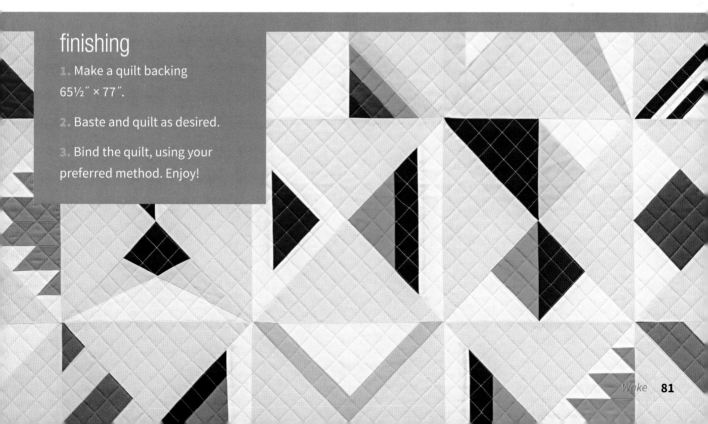

twilight

Finished quilt: 62″ × 73½″   ▲   Finished triangle: 8″

This quilt plays with the much-loved Flying Geese block. The graphic triangle blocks bring boldness to the geese, and the change in background color further enlivens the design.

There are 38 possible geese for you to fill with right triangle blocks in the quilt as shown, but you can make up to 44 Flying Geese / right triangle combos if desired. Mix in some base triangles and Half-Base blocks to add large hunks of color and a place for the eye to rest.

Materials

Black (Kona Pepper): ½ yard

Blue-green (Kona Jade Green): 1 yard

Light blue-green (Kona Candy Green): 1 yard

Light green (Kona Pond): 1 yard

Yellow-green (Kona Wasabi): 1 yard

White (Kona Snow): 2⅞ yards

Backing: 4 yards

Batting: 70″ × 82″

Binding: ⅝ yard

Background Cutting

You need 2 half-square triangles for each Flying Geese block—76 total for this layout. Feel free to change up the quantities of each color to suit your design.

BLUE-GREEN

• Cut 2 strips 6⅝″ × fabric width. Subcut into 8 squares 6⅝″ × 6⅝″. Cut each square in half diagonally to yield 16 triangles.

LIGHT BLUE-GREEN

• Cut 2 strips 6⅝″ × fabric width. Subcut into 7 squares 6⅝″ × 6⅝″. Cut each square in half diagonally to yield 14 triangles.

LIGHT GREEN

• Cut 2 strips 6⅝″ × fabric width. Subcut into 8 squares 6⅝″ × 6⅝″. Cut each square in half diagonally to yield 16 triangles.

YELLOW-GREEN

• Cut 2 strips 6⅝″ × fabric width. Subcut into 8 squares 6⅝″ × 6⅝″. Cut each square in half diagonally to yield 16 triangles.

WHITE

• Cut 3 strips 11¾″ × fabric width.

• Cut 2 strips 6⅝″ × fabric width. Subcut into 7 squares 6⅝″ × 6⅝″. Cut each square in half diagonally to yield 14 triangles.

• Cut 4 strips 8½″ × fabric width.

• Cut 3 strips 2½″ × fabric width.

piecing

1. Use the right triangle block instructions (page 59) to make up to 38 right triangle blocks. I made 24 right triangle blocks and used 13 base triangles and 1 Half-Base block. I chose Blocks 1–19.

2. Refer to the quilt assembly diagram (page 84) to lay out your blocks and base triangles in 4 columns on a design surface. Play with the overall layout of the blocks, balancing the contrast and color placement.

3. If you want background rectangles between the Flying Geese blocks, cut 6¼″ × 11¾″ rectangles from a 11¾″-wide white strip and place them now. I used 2 rectangles, 1 at the top of one column and 1 at the bottom (C).

4. Cut the 2 remaining white 11¾″-wide strips in half through the width and arrange as desired at the top and bottom of the Flying Geese columns (A and B). These will be trimmed down later.

5. Sew a background triangle to the left side of each of the right triangle blocks. Press the seam toward the background.

6. Sew another background triangle to the right side of each right triangle block to make a Flying Geese block. Press the seam toward the background.

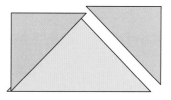

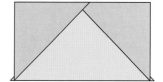

assembling the quilt top

1. Sew the Flying Geese blocks and any interior white rectangles together in columns. Add the larger white strips at the tops and bottoms of the columns, following your layout. Press the seams in alternating directions: In rows 1 and 3, press the seams up. In rows 2 and 4, press the seams down.

2. Trim all 4 columns to the same height (or the height of 12 Flying Geese blocks, if you have a column without background fabric at the top and bottom).

3. Sew the columns together, pinning the intersections of the Flying Geese blocks to align them. Press the seams as desired.

4. Sew the 2½˝ white strips together end to end to form 1 long strip. Press the seams to one side. Measure the quilt horizontally through the center and cut 2 strips to fit.

5. Sew the 2½˝-wide strips to the top and bottom of the center panel. Press the seams toward the 2½˝ strips.

6. Sew the 8½˝ strips together end to end to form 1 long strip. Press the seams to one side. Measure the quilt vertically through the center and cut 2 strips to fit.

7. Sew the 8½˝-wide strips to the sides of the center panel. Press the seams toward the 8½˝ strips.

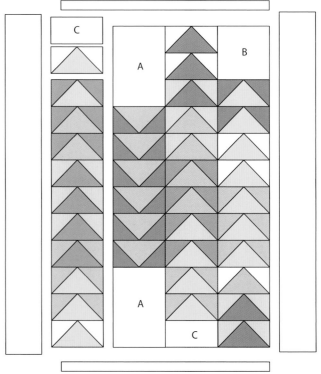

Quilt assembly

finishing

1. Make a quilt backing 70˝ × 81˝

2. Baste and quilt as desired.

3. Bind the quilt, using your preferred method. Enjoy!

isosceles triangles

This section covers isosceles triangle blocks and quilts. An isosceles triangle is a triangle with two equal sides and two equal angles. The blocks themselves are designed to play simply with each other. The piecing isn't complicated; the challenge is in the unusual angle.

Following the instructions on how to make the isosceles base blocks, there are fourteen block patterns. Techniques rely mostly on strip piecing, paper piecing, and using the isosceles triangle trimming templates (pattern pullout pages P2 and P3).

After the block patterns, you'll find three quilt projects that play with the simplicity of the blocks in repetition. One quilt maxes out on triangles. One allows you to use a small number of triangle blocks but still get a sizable quilt. I'll list the blocks I used in each pattern, but please choose whichever blocks you love.

special notes

COLOR PALETTE

I chose a navy and peach color palette for this section. Within each color, I used a few variations. This way I could add color and texture without straying too much from my palette.

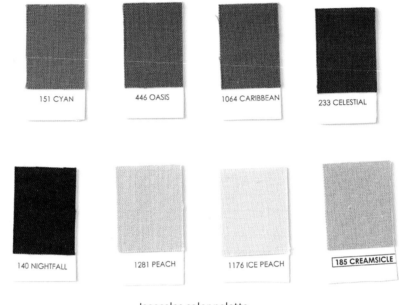

151 CYAN 446 OASIS 1064 CARIBBEAN 233 CELESTIAL

140 NIGHTFALL 1281 PEACH 1176 ICE PEACH 185 CREAMSICLE

Isosceles color palette

TRIANGLE SIZES

Quilt projects in this section use either the 6″ or 12″ isosceles triangles. The sampler uses 12″ finished isosceles triangles, and therefore, the block patterns are written for the 12″ size. Cutting instructions for the 6″ finished isosceles triangles can be found in the sizing options for each block.

TIP **Important Takeaway**

When I refer to the "size" of the isosceles triangle, I mean the finished height (either 6″ or 12″) of the triangle.

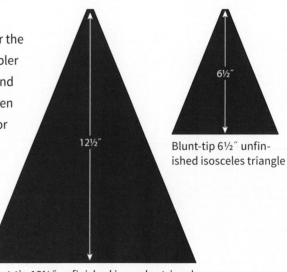

6½″

Blunt-tip 6½″ unfinished isosceles triangle

12½″

Blunt-tip 12½″ unfinished isosceles triangle

Size = triangle height

isosceles triangle blocks

isosceles triangle blocks (Base–Block 14)

Make a copy of this page and use it as a planning sheet while you make your project.

Base block

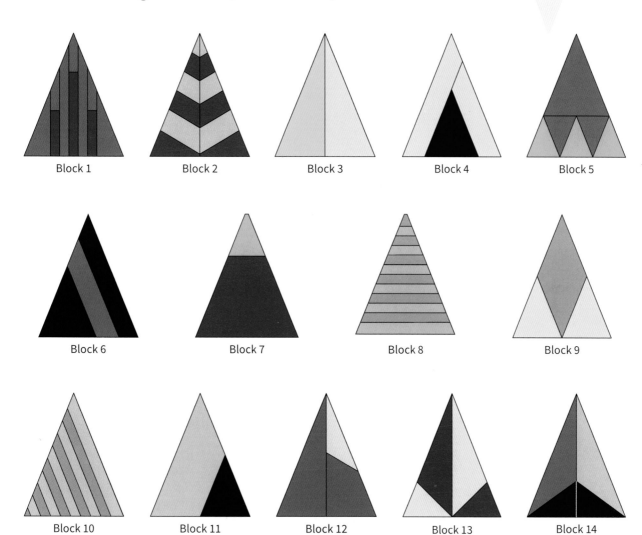

Block 1

Block 2

Block 3

Block 4

Block 5

Block 6

Block 7

Block 8

Block 9

Block 10

Block 11

Block 12

Block 13

Block 14

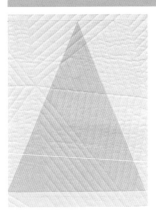

Isosceles Base Triangle

BASE BLOCK

Use Base blocks for a large splash of color or a place for the eye to rest.
The quilt projects rely heavily on the Base block for quilt-top construction.

Cutting Several Isosceles Triangles from Yardage

Cut fabric widths equaling the height of the unfinished blunt-tip triangle. For example, if you are using 12″ isosceles triangle blocks, cut a strip that is 12½″ × fabric width. Unfold the fabric width and use the 12″ isosceles triangle trimming template (pattern pullout page P2) to cut several triangles.

Cutting isosceles triangles from a strip

Cutting 1 Isosceles Triangle

Cut a rectangle 11″ × 12½″. Use the 12″ isosceles triangle trimming template to trace the pattern, and then cut along the traced lines.

Cutting 1 isosceles
triangle at a time

Cut a rectangle 5¾″ × 6½″. Use the 6″ isosceles triangle trimming template to trace the pattern, and then cut along the traced lines.

Block 1

Block Stats

- Strip piecing
- Trimming template

Materials and Cutting for 12″ Isosceles Triangles

- **Dark blue:** 1 strip 1½″ × 9″

  2 strips 1½″ × 5″

- **Light blue:** 2 strips 1½″ × 11½″

  3 strips 1½″ × 6″

  2 rectangles 4″ × 8″

- **Trimming template:** 12″ isosceles triangle
  (pattern pullout page P2)

PIECING

1. Sew the dark blue strip 1½″ × 9″ to a light blue strip 1½″ × 6″. Sew the 2 dark blue strips 1½″ × 5″ to the other 2 light blue strips 1½″ × 5″. Press the seams toward the dark blue.

2. Lay out and sew all the strips together, aligning the bottom edges. Press.

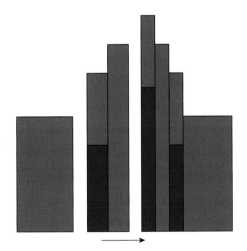

3. Center and trace the isosceles triangle trimming template (pattern pullout page P2). Cut along the traced lines.

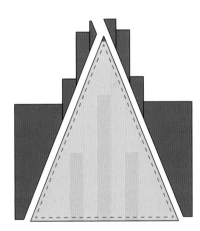

Sizing Option

	Materials and cutting for 6″ isosceles triangle
Dark blue	1 strip 1″ × 5″
	2 strips 1″ × 3″
Light blue	2 strips 1″ × 6½″
	3 strips 1″ × 3½″
	2 rectangles 2″ × 4″
Trimming template	6″ isosceles triangle (pattern pullout page P3)

Block 2

Block Stats

- Strip piecing
- Trimming template

Materials and Cutting for 12″ Isosceles Triangle

- **Dark blue:** 4 strips 2⅜″ × 6″

  2 strips 4″ × 6½″

- **Peach:** 4 strips 2⅜″ × 6″

  2 strips 4″ × 6½″

- **Trimming template:** 12″ isosceles triangle (pattern pullout page P2)

PIECING

1. Piece the strips together, alternating the colors, and put the wider strips at the ends to make 2 strip sets, as shown. Stagger the strips in the first strip set about 1″ up from the previous strip and in the second about 1″ down from the previous strip.

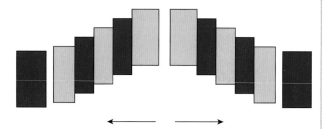

2. Align the 30° line on your acrylic ruler with one of the seams in the strip set and trim the right side. Repeat with the other strip set, but trim the left side.

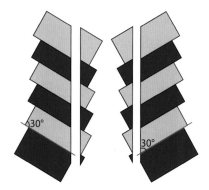

3. Sew the pieces together along the cut edges. Press the seams open.

4. Center and trace the isosceles triangle trimming template, aligning the bottom "V" with the ¼″ seam allowance. Cut along the traced lines.

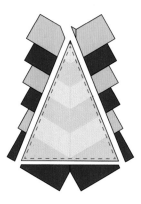

Sizing Option

	Materials and cutting for 6″ isosceles triangle
Dark blue	4 strips 1½″ × 3¼″
	2 strips 2¼″ × 3¾″
Peach	4 strips 1½″ × 3¼″
	2 strips 2¼″ × 3¾″
Trimming template	6″ isosceles triangle (pattern pullout page P3)

Block 3

Block Stats

• Piecing

• **Peach:** 1 piece, using the 12″ half-isosceles triangle trimming template (pattern pullout page P2)

• **Light peach:** 1 piece, using the 12″ half-isosceles triangle trimming template (pattern pullout page P2)*

For patterned fabric, flip the template upside down.

PIECING

1. Sew the 2 pieces together along the long edges. Press the seam to one side.

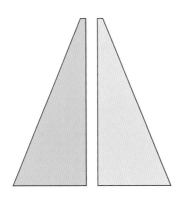

Sizing Option

	Materials and cutting for 6″ isosceles triangle
Peach	1 piece, using the 6″ half-isosceles triangle trimming template (pattern pullout page P1)
Light peach	1 piece, using the 6″ half-isosceles triangle trimming template (pattern pullout page P1)*

For patterned fabric, flip the template upside down.

Block 4

Block Stats

- Piecing
- Trimming template

Materials and Cutting for 12″ Isosceles Triangle

- **Navy:** 1 square 8″ × 8″
- **Peach:** 1 strip 2½″ × 13″ and 1 strip 2½″ × 15″
- **Trimming template:** 12″ isosceles triangle (pattern pullout page P2)

PIECING

1. Use the 12″ isosceles triangle trimming template (pattern pullout page P2) to cut an isosceles triangle from the navy square, as shown.

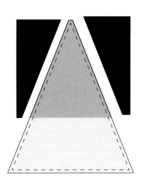

2. Sew the 13″ peach strip, centered, to the right side of the triangle. Press the seam to the side. Trim the excess fabric away.

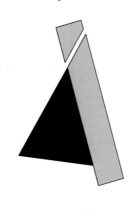

3. Sew the 15″ peach strip to the left side, making sure that the majority of extra fabric is at the top of the triangle. Press the seam to the side.

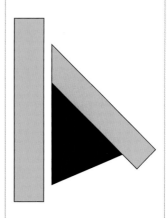

4. Trace around the isosceles triangle trimming template (pattern pullout page P2) and cut along the traced lines.

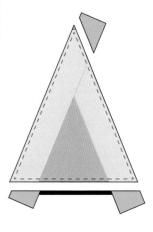

Sizing Option

	Materials and cutting for 6″ isosceles triangle
Navy	1 square 4″ × 4″
Peach	1 strip 1½″ × 7″ and 1 strip 1½″ × 8″
Trimming template	6″ isosceles triangle (pattern pullout page P3)

Block 5

Block Stats

- Piecing
- Trimming template

Materials and Cutting for 12″ Isosceles Triangle

- **Blue:** 2 squares 4½″ × 4½″

  1 square 8½″ × 8½″
- **Peach:** 3 squares 4½″ × 4½″
- **Trimming template:** 12″ isosceles triangle (pattern pullout page P2)

PIECING

1. Use the isosceles triangle trimming template to cut 2 triangles from the 4½″ × 4½″ squares and 1 triangle from the 8½″ × 8½″ square.

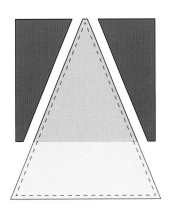

2. Sew the small triangles together, alternating the colors. Press the seams open.

3. Add the 8½″ blue isosceles triangle to the top. Press the seam to the top.

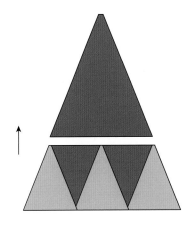

Sizing Option

	Materials and cutting for 6″ isosceles triangle (The 6″ version is better paper pieced.)
Blue	Scraps
Peach	Scraps
Foundation pattern	6″ isosceles triangle Block 5 (pattern pullout page P3)

Block 6

Block Stats

- Piecing
- Trimming template

Materials and Cutting for 12″ Isosceles Triangle

- **Navy:** 1 square 8″ × 8″ and 1 strip 2½″ × 16″
- **Turquoise:** 1 strip 2½″ × 13″
- **Trimming template:** 12″ isosceles triangle (pattern pullout page P2)

PIECING

1. Use the isosceles triangle trimming template to cut an isosceles triangle from the navy square 8″ × 8″, as shown.

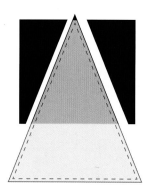

2. Sew the turquoise strip to the right of the isosceles triangle. Press the seam to one side and trim.

3. Sew the navy strip to the right of the turquoise strip. Press the seam to one side.

4. Trace around the isosceles triangle trimming template (pattern pullout page P2) and cut along the traced lines.

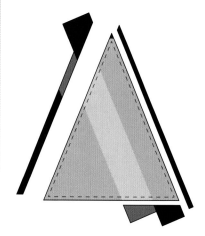

Sizing Option

	Materials and cutting for 6″ isosceles triangle
Navy	1 square 4½″ × 4½″ and 1 strip 1½″ × 9″
Turquoise	1 strip 1½″ × 7″
Trimming template	6″ isosceles triangle (pattern pullout page P3)

Block 7

Block Stats

- Piecing
- Trimming template

Materials and Cutting for 12″ Isosceles Triangle

- **Peach:** 1 square 5″ × 5″
- **Blue:** 1 rectangle 8½″ × 12″
- **Trimming template:** 12″ isosceles triangle (pattern pullout page P2)

PIECING

1. Sew the rectangles as shown, aligning the centers. Press the seam to one side.

2. Center and trace the isosceles triangle trimming template (pattern pullout page P2). Cut along the traced lines.

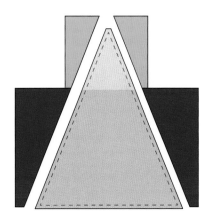

Sizing Option

	Materials and cutting for 6″ isosceles triangle
Peach	1 square 3″ × 3″
Blue	1 rectangle 4½″ × 6″
Trimming template	6″ isosceles triangle (pattern pullout page P3)

Block 8

Block Stats

- Strip piecing
- Trimming template

Materials and Cutting for 12″ Isosceles Triangle

- **Peach:** 6 strips 1½″ × 11″
- **Turquoise:** 5 strips 1½″ × 11″

  1 strip 2½″ × 11″
- **Trimming template:** 12″ isosceles triangle (pattern pullout page P2)

PIECING

1. Sew the strips together, alternating colors. Note that the 2½″ strip needs to be at the top, where the point will be. Press the seams as desired.

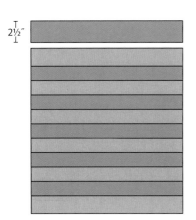

2. Trace around the isosceles triangle trimming template (pattern pullout page P2) and cut along the traced lines.

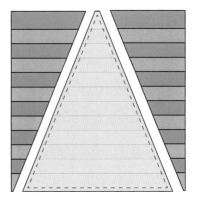

Sizing Option

	Materials and cutting for 6″ isosceles triangle
Peach	6 strips 1″ × 6″
Turquoise	5 strips 1″ × 6″
	1 strip 2″ × 6″
Trimming template	6″ isosceles triangle (pattern pullout page P3)

Note: To make the 6″ block more manageable, you may want to use 3 strips 2½″ × 6″ instead of the 6 strips 1″ × 6″.

Block 9

Block Stats

- Piecing
- Trimming template

Materials and Cutting for 12″ Isosceles Triangle

- **Peach:** 2 squares 6½″ × 6½″
- **Turquoise:** 1 piece, using the 12″ isosceles triangle Block 9 template (pattern pullout page P3)
- **Trimming template:** 12″ isosceles triangle (pattern pullout page P2)

PIECING

1. Use the isosceles triangle trimming template to cut a 6½″ isosceles triangle from each of the peach squares, as shown.

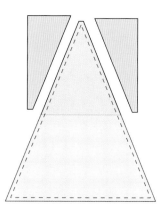

2. Add the peach triangles on the lower left and right sides of the turquoise piece. Press the seams away from the center.

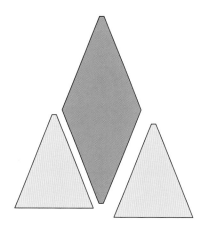

Sizing Option

	Materials and cutting for 6″ isosceles triangle
Peach	2 squares 3½″ × 3½″
Turquoise	1 piece, using the 6″ isosceles triangle Block 9 template (pattern pullout page P1)
Trimming template	6″ isosceles triangle (pattern pullout page P3)
In Step 1:	Use the isosceles triangle trimming template to cut an isosceles triangle from each square 3½″ × 3½″.

Block 10

Block Stats

- Strip piecing
- Trimming template

Materials and Cutting for 12″ Isosceles Triangle

- **Turquoise:** 5 strips 1½″ × 14″
- **Peach:** 5 strips 1½″ × 14″
- **Trimming template:** 12″ isosceles triangle (pattern pullout page P2)

PIECING

1. Sew the fabric strips together, alternating colors. Press the seams as desired.

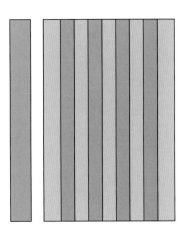

2. Align a long side of the isosceles triangle trimming template (pattern pullout page P2) on the right. Trace around the template and cut along the traced lines.

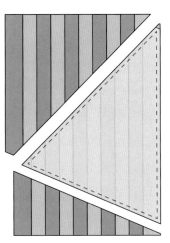

Sizing Option

	Materials and cutting for 6″ isosceles triangle
Turquoise	5 strips 1″ × 7½″
Peach	5 strips 1″ × 7½″
Trimming template	6″ isosceles triangle (pattern pullout page P3)

Block 11

Block Stats

- Piecing

Materials and Cutting

- **Peach:** 1 piece, using the 12″ isosceles triangle Block 11 template (pattern pullout page P3)

- **Navy:** 1 square 6½″ × 6½″

- **Trimming template:** 12″ isosceles triangle (pattern pullout page P2)

PIECING

1. Use the isosceles triangle trimming template (pattern pullout page P2) to cut an isosceles triangle from the navy square, as shown.

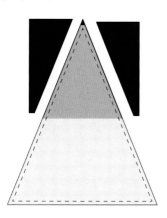

2. Sew the navy triangle to the peach piece. Press the seam as desired.

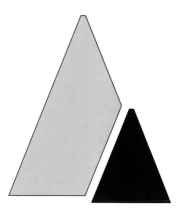

Sizing Option

	Materials and cutting for 6″ isosceles triangle
Peach	1 piece, using the 6″ isosceles triangle Block 11 template (pattern pullout page P3)
Navy	1 square 3½″ × 3½″
Trimming template	6″ isosceles triangle (pattern pullout page P3)
In Step 1:	Use the 6″ isosceles triangle trimming template to cut an isosceles triangle.

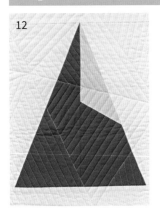

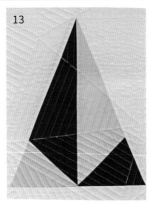

Block Stats

• Paper piecing

Materials and Cutting for 12″ Isosceles Triangle

• **Fabric scraps:** assorted

• **Dark blue:** 1 half-isosceles 12″ triangle (pattern pullout page P2) for Block 12

• **Pattern:** a copy of the desired 12″ isosceles block foundation pattern (pullout pages P2 and P3)

PIECING

1. Paper piece each block using the corresponding foundation patterns.

2. For Block 12, sew the paper-pieced foundation pattern to the dark blue half-isosceles triangle. Press the seam to the side.

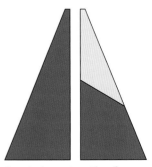

Sew 2 pieces together for Block 12.

Sizing Option

	Materials and cutting for 6″ isosceles triangle
Fabric scraps	Assorted
Dark blue	1 half-isosceles 6″ triangle (pattern pullout page P1) for Block 12
Pattern	A copy of the desired 6″ isosceles block foundation pattern (pullout pages P1 and P3)

isosceles sampler

Finished quilt: 54½″ × 64½″ ▲ Finished triangle: 12″

With this sampler you can make one of each of the isosceles blocks and end up with a big and bold quilt. At 12″, the finished triangles come together to create a nice throw quilt. Increase the borders for a larger quilt. By using the 6″ triangles, you could make a bold little quilt finishing at 28½″ × 31½″.

Materials

Dark blue (Kona Nightfall): ½ yard

Dark peach (Kona Creamsicle): ½ yard

Dark teal (Kona Celestial): ½ yard

Light peach (Kona Ice Peach): ½ yard

Sea blue (Kona Oasis): ½ yard

Turquoise (Kona Cyan): ½ yard

White (Kona White): 3 yards

Backing: 3⅝ yards

Batting: 62½″ × 72½″

Binding: ⅝ yard

Background Cutting

WHITE

- Cut 3 strips 12½″ × fabric width. Using the 12″ half-isosceles triangle trimming template (pattern pullout page P2), cut 30 half-isosceles triangles.

- Cut 5 strips 2½″ × fabric width.

- Cut 2 length-of-fabric strips 12½″ × 54½″.

piecing

TRIANGLES

Use the isosceles triangle block instructions (page 87) to make 1 of each block. Make 1 extra block—or do what I did, and cut a base triangle—for a total of 15 blocks.

PIECING

1. Sew a half-isosceles triangle to the left of each isosceles block. Press the seam to the side.

2. Sew a half-isosceles triangle to the right side of each isosceles block. Press the seam to the side.

assembling the quilt top

1. Lay out the isosceles blocks on a design surface. Consider color, contrast, and balance as you work toward the final composition. I rotated every other block.

2. Sew the isosceles blocks together into rows. Press the seams as desired.

3. Sew 3 white 2½″ strips together end to end to make 1 long strip. Press the seams as desired. Cut into 2 strips 2½″ × 50½″.

4. Add these strips to the top of the bottom and middle rows. Press the seams toward the sashing strips.

5. Sew the rows together. Press the seams toward the sashing strips.

6. Measure the center panel vertically through the middle. Cut the remaining 2 white 2½″ × fabric width strips to fit.

7. Sew the trimmed 2½″ white strips to each side of the center panel. Press the seams toward the strips.

8. Repeat Steps 6 and 7 to measure and add the 12½″-wide strips to the bottom and top of the center panel. Press the seams toward the strips.

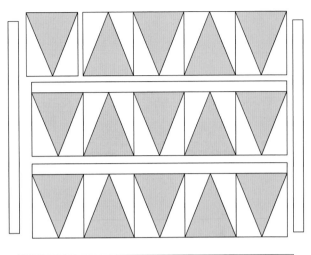

Quilt assembly

finishing

1. Make a quilt backing 62½″ × 72½″.

2. Baste and quilt as desired.

3. Bind the quilt, using your preferred method. Enjoy!

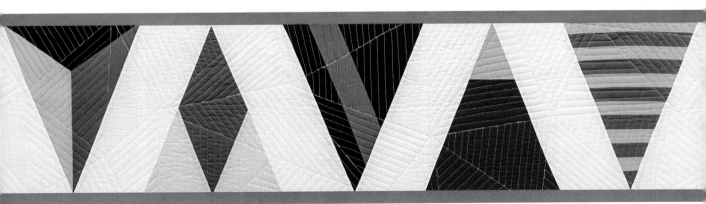

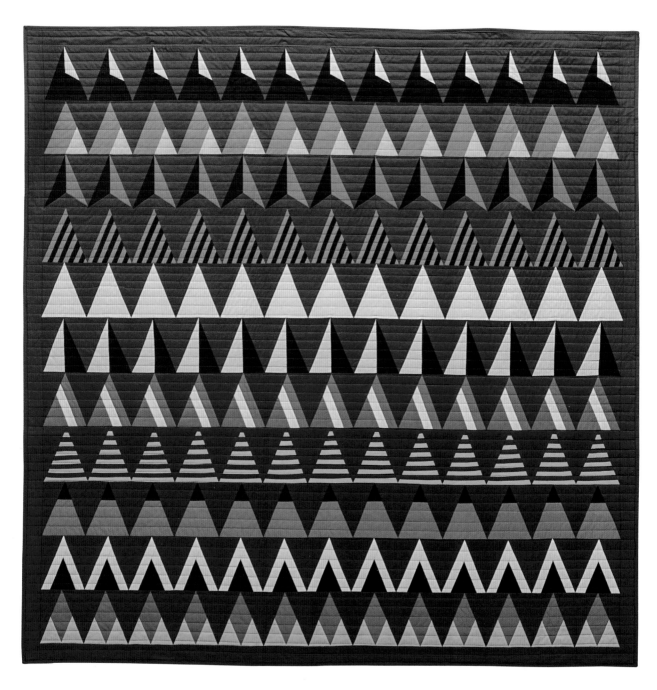

riptide

Finished quilt: 69½″ × 70½″ ▲ Finished triangle: 6″

This quilt plays with the notion of simple but bold repeating patterns. Each block is repeated across the width of the quilt. Play with color or change up the intensity of block. For example, you could make a smaller number of blocks and arrange them randomly amongst the solid background triangles.

Materials

Dark blue (Kona Nightfall): 1 yard

Dark peach (Kona Creamsicle): 1 yard

Dark turquoise (Kona Caribbean): 1 yard

Light peach (Kona Ice Peach): 1 yard

Peach (Kona Peach): 1 yard

Sea blue (Kona Oasis): 1 yard

Turquoise (Kona Cyan): 1 yard

Dark teal (Kona Celestial): 3½ yards

Backing: 4⅝ yards

Batting: 77½″ × 78½″

Binding: ⅝ yard

Background Cutting

DARK TEAL

- Cut 12 strips 6½″ × fabric width. Using the 6″ isosceles triangle trimming template (pattern pullout page P3), cut 12 triangles from each strip.

- Cut 1 strip 6½″ × fabric width. Cut 22 half triangles, using the 6″ half-isosceles triangle trimming template (pattern pullout page P1).

- Cut 7 strips 2½″ × fabric width.

piecing

TRIANGLES

Use the 6″ isosceles triangle block instructions (page 87) to make 13 each of your 11 favorite blocks. I chose the Base block and Blocks 3, 4, 6–12, and 14.

assembling the quilt top

1. Lay out the blocks, background triangles, and half-isosceles triangles to decide the final composition.

2. Begin assembling the rows by sewing the triangles into pairs. Each pair should be 1 block and 1 background triangle. Press the seams as desired. (There will be a leftover block.)

3. Finish the rows by sewing the pairs together, adding the half-isosceles triangles at the ends. Press the seams as desired.

4. Sew the rows together. Press as desired.

5. Measure the quilt top vertically through the middle.

6. Sew the 2½″ strips together to make 1 long strip. Press the seams to the side. From this long strip, cut 2 strips to fit.

7. Sew the strips to the left and right sides of the quilt top. Press the seams toward the border.

8. Measure the quilt top horizontally through the middle. Cut the remaining long 2½″ strip into 2 strips to fit.

9. Sew the strips to the top and bottom of the quilt top. Press the seams toward the border.

Quilt assembly

finishing

1. Make a quilt backing 77½″ × 78½″.

2. Baste and quilt as desired.

3. Bind the quilt, using your preferred method. Enjoy!

stardust

Finished quilt: 62½″ × 72½″ ▲ Finished triangle: 12″

This quilt shows a modern arrangement of 12″ finished isosceles triangles with a graphic twist. My quilt shows 23 graphic pieced triangle blocks, but there are a possible 33 triangles to create as isosceles triangle blocks. You might also like to play with the 6 half-triangles at the right border to carry the design off the edge.

For a baby quilt, the blocks can be scaled to 6″ using the sizing options given in each block.

Materials

Black (Kona Pepper): ½ yard

Dark peach (Kona Creamsicle): ½ yard

Dark teal (Kona Celestial): ½ yard

Dark turquoise (Kona Caribbean): ½ yard

Pale gray (Kona Silver): ½ yard

Light peach (Kona Ice Peach): ½ yard

Medium gray (Kona Graphite): ½ yard

Peach (Kona Peach): ½ yard

Turquoise (Kona Cyan): ½ yard

Dark blue (Kona Nightfall): 2½ yards

Backing: 4⅝ yards

Batting: 70½″ × 80½″

Binding: ⅝ yard

Background Cutting

DARK BLUE

• Cut 6 strips 12½″ × fabric width. Set aside 3 strips for rows 1, 2, and 3.

  Trim 1 strip to 12½″ × 32″ for row 4.

  Trim 2 strips to 12½″ × 28″ for rows 5 and 6.

(Save the trimmed-off pieces to add to rows 1 and 2 when assembling the quilt top.)

piecing

TRIANGLES

1. Use the isosceles triangle block instructions (page 87) to make up to 33 of your favorite blocks. I made multiples of some blocks and used 9 base triangles.

2. Cut 6 half-isosceles base triangles, using the 12″ half-isosceles triangle trimming template (pattern pullout page P2).

assembling the quilt top

1. Refer to the quilt assembly diagram to lay out your isosceles triangle blocks and Base blocks on a design surface in rows. Decide on your final layout. As you work with the composition, consider color placement and contrast.

2. Lengthen the background fabric strips for rows 1 and 2 by sewing the longer background scrap to the row 1 strip and one of the shorter scraps to the row 2 strip. Press the seams to the side.

3. Referring to the quilt assembly diagram, trim the right-hand end of the background strips using the 12″ isosceles triangle trimming template, as shown.

For rows 4 and 5, be sure to flip the template to get the angle you need. This is especially important if you are using printed fabric.

4. Begin assembling the rows by sewing the triangles into pairs. Press the seams as desired.

5. Finish the rows by sewing the pairs together. Then add the angled background strips to the left-hand side of the rows. Press the seams as desired.

6. Sew the rows together. Press as desired.

7. Trim the left side of the quilt top even with the top row.

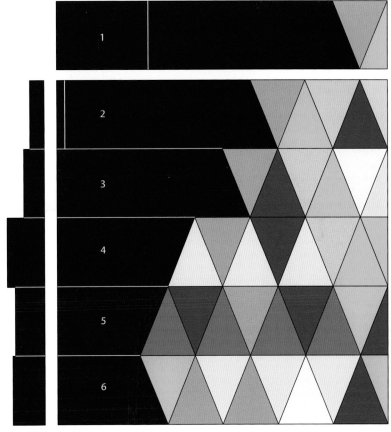

Quilt assembly

▶▶

finish

1. Make a quilt backing 70½″ × 80½″.

2. Baste and quilt as desired.

3. Bind the quilt, using your preferred method. Enjoy!

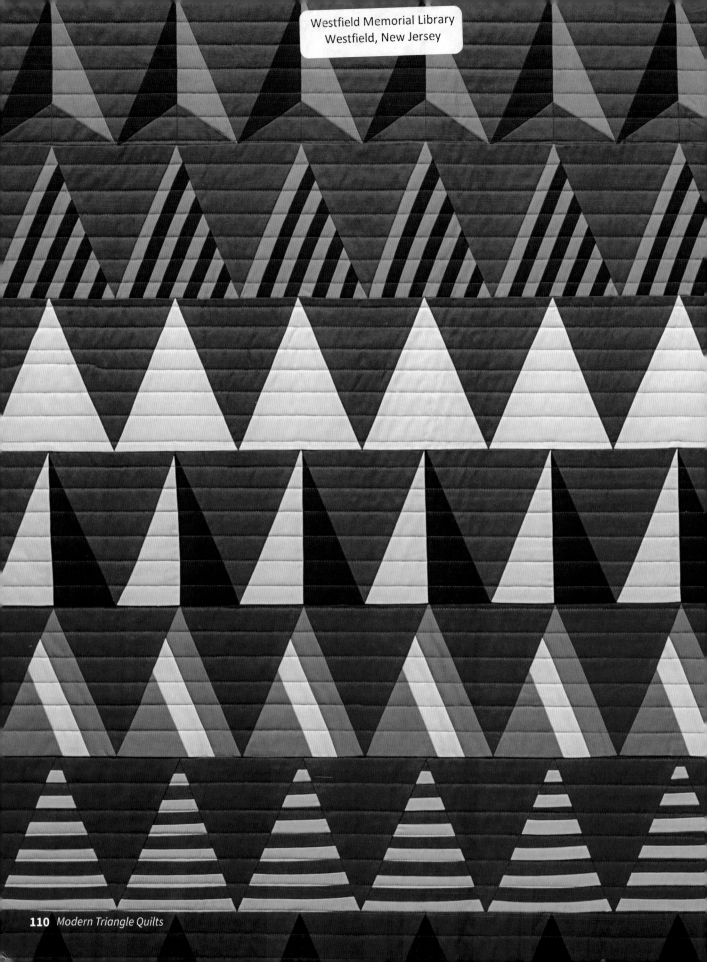

about the author

Having grown up around quiltmaking, Rebecca has always found inspiration in traditional designs and classical piecing techniques. After making her first official quilt for her first official apartment in college, Rebecca began to explore modern and improvisational quiltmaking. The journey led Rebecca to discover her voice as a maker.

Rebecca's love of color is best exemplified in her first book, *Modern Rainbow: 14 Imaginative Quilts That Play with Color*, which debuted in 2015. Rebecca believes firmly in the power of color as a driver of creativity. If it's not colorful, don't do it.

One of the best things about quiltmaking is that makers each create what they love using their favorite colors, techniques, or patterns. Therefore, Rebecca's favorite patterns to write are those that allow the maker's personality to shine through.

Rebecca lives in St. Louis, Missouri, with her husband, four children, and two dogs. You can find more about Rebecca and her quilts by visiting her blog, bryanhousequilts.com.

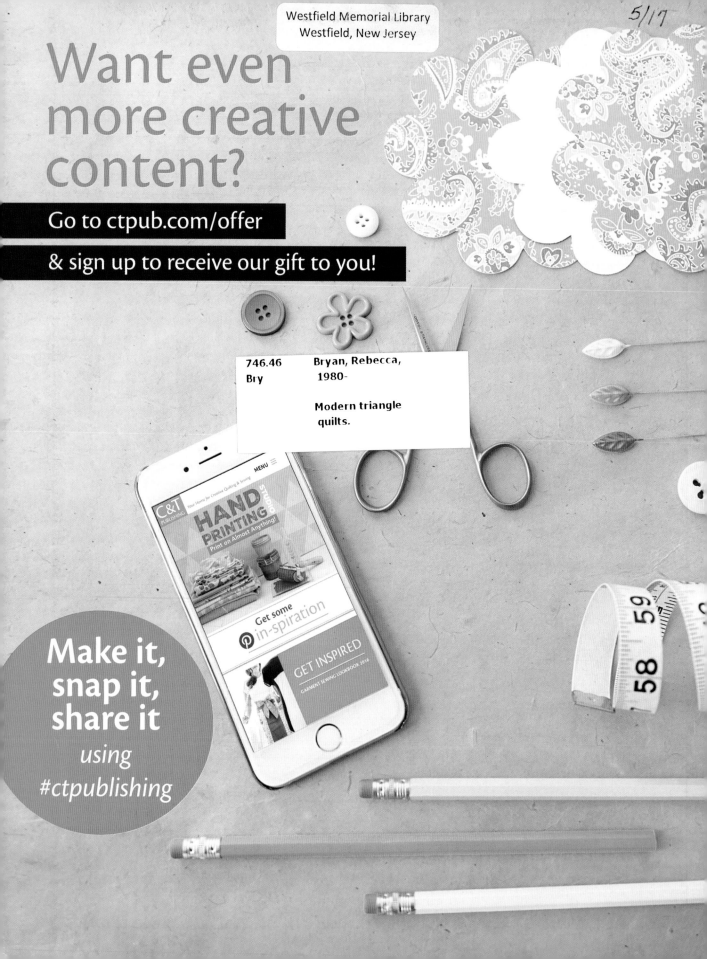

Want even more creative content?

Go to ctpub.com/offer

& sign up to receive our gift to you!

Make it, snap it, share it
using
#ctpublishing

TRIUMPH
ENTERTAINMENT

Credits

This book is not sponsored, endorsed by, or otherwise affiliated with any companies or the products feature in this book.   This is not an official publication.

Editor in Chief – Bill Gill, A.K.A. "Pojo"
Creative Director & Graphic Design – Jon Anderson
Publisher – Bob Baker
Contributors – Amy Gill, Kym Huynh, Scott Gerhardt, DeQuan Watson, Paul Hagan and Matt Murphy

Kym Huynh and our staff also wish to offer a sincere thank-you to the following people who voluntarily contributed artwork:

Artists: Katie Hartman; Kismet; Krista Nicholson; Megan Cubbage; Nicole Emery

Neopets is an Amazing Phenomenon!!!

Neopets is an interesting phenomenon. I mean, there's no way a product like Neopets could have even existed before 1995 or so, because the World Wide Web really didn't exist in full force until the late 1990's. Neopets.com started in 1997, and in 6 short years it has grown astronomically. Nearly every kid and teenager that surfs the net knows what Neopets are. According to Alexa.com, Neopets.com is the 55th most popular website in the world.

(I also want to toss in the fact that the fine folks at Neopets advertised on Pojo.com in 1999 to tap into our huge Pokemon audience at the time. Maybe we can take a smidgeon of credit for its incredible growth).

I started playing Neopets online last year. I really had trouble getting started at first. I couldn't log in after signing up! Then I figured out that I had to turn off Norton Internet Security before logging in. If you are having trouble getting started, maybe it's your firewall. :-P

I currently have two online pets, a Red Scorchio which I adopted, and a Red Grarrl. My favorite games are "Spell or Starve" and "Word Poker". It's also fun to play the "Extreme Potato Counter" with a handful of people and have everyone watch a different part of the screen and see how far you can get.

Moving on. In the fall of 2003, Wizards of the Coast, the king of Trading Card Games, came out with a Neopets Trading Card Game. If you haven't played it yet, it's a really fun game. It's easy to learn, and a gas to play. Plus every Neopets trading card game booster pack contains a Virtual Prize Code redeemable at neopets.com for a chance at exclusive virtual items, Neopoints, and more! Some people collect the trading cards, and then sell the prize code cards on EBay. We've seen 10 prize codes go for $31 on eBay. That's unbelievable to me. Though I always use my codes as opposed to selling them.

Anyways, late in 2003 our publisher asked us to come with a Neopets book on short notice for the holidays. Of course we jumped at the chance. We broke the book up into two sections. The first section deals with the online Neopets world. And the second section deals with the Trading Card Game. We've assembled some of the best & brightest people and players in the world to help create this book. We hope you enjoy reading this as much as we enjoyed creating it. Please forgive us for any spelling errors this time around, as we really rushed to get this book into your hands. ;-)

Pojo

Pojo

P.S. Special thanks to all the talented artists who volunteered to provide us with artwork to use inside the book. That was really cool of you.

Neopets Table of Contents

Online Pets:

The Trading Card Game

Pg 32: Card Reviews

Scott Gerhardt is a Pro Tour Magic: The Gathering Player. Scott was also regarded as one of the best Pokemon players in the world back in his heyday. Now Scott's reviewing every single card in the Neopets Trading Card Game at the present time. All 240 cards are reviewed individually for you here. This is pretty darn cool.

Pg 57: Killer Decks

Four different deck designers have four different deck ideas for you. And they teach you what goes into to making a Killer Deck.

Pg 65: Luck or Skill

Are the good players just lucky? Or is there something more to it?

Pg 67: Green Neggs and Ham

DeQuan Watson reviews all the Neggs in this first set. Can you make an all Neggs deck?

Pg 69: Banking vs. Decking

Learn whether it's the proper time in the game to bank or draw cards.

Pg 71: Make it a combo!

Scott Gerhardt discusses some of the Killer Combos that you can try to create while making your deck.

Pg 73: Top 5 Lists and Top 10 Lists

DeQuan Watson has a couple handfuls of Lists of his favorite cards for you!

Exploring the World of Neopia

By: Kym Huynh

Welcome to the world of Neopets! I am Kym, a Neopets player who has experienced nearly everything that there is to experience in this game. This section contains a wealth of information for you to uncover and read!

Dragonsheir
Artwork by Katie Hartman

Special Thanks To PPT www.pinkpt.com for their contribution and help!

As many of you may know, Neopets is a game of magic and excitement, where any decision you make will affect other aspects of your Neopian life. This world is filled with friends to make. On the other hand, it is also plagued with scammers and scoundrels, who would like to do nothing better than to rob you of your achievements. In my opinion, the risks are worth it! This game, other than its entertainment value, has been an invaluable educational experience for me. From its scammers and hackers, I have learned that the world is not a perfect place. Through its integrated commerce system, I have learned the real value of money. Through its stock market, auctions and trading, I have learned valuable commerce and haggling skills. These things cannot be learned in the classroom. I am thankful that I was able to learn them in a simulated environment rather than learning them in the real world, where the results could become nasty. Are you willing to also learn these things?

Your Neopets journey will depend on the decisions you make at every crossroad. Will you become the richest Neopian? Will you aim to raise the strongest Neopet in

existence? Will you aim to collect all the items that exist in Neopia to show off in your gallery? Or do you plan to hoard all the available trophies for everyone to marvel at? Whatever you decide, Neopets is wrought with fun, excitement, and it's fair share of dangers, which you will hopefully avoid. Alongside your Neopet companions, your journey will hopefully be a joyous one.

Keep in mind that every step you take will take you closer to your goals, no matter how big or small the step is. Even if you are an experienced player, this section of the book will hopefully give you insight into the world you play in.

Neopets is a game, which has no clear ending. Like many simulation games, there is no winning point, and the game only ends when you have chosen to end it. Any goal, which you choose to make, will determine how long you will play the game. Keep this book handy because it will aid you in your endeavors! Whatever you choose, good luck and happy Neopetting!

-- Kym

This section of the book is dedicated to my family and friends. I also extend a warm hand to the tremendous people at PPT (http://www.pinkpt.com) for making my Neopian experience a joyful one. Your crazy antics, random but intelligent conversations and supportive community nature have been a joyous ray of light.

Questions, Comments, Suggestions

If you have any questions, comments, or suggestions please email me knphuynh@hotmail.com ●

In the Beginning

By: Kym Huynh

A long time ago in a land far, far away in the year of 1998, two college buddies notoriously known as Adam and Donna set out to create an online world of wonder, intrigue, magic and excitement. They didn't know that this world would one day become one of the most talked about worlds. Gracing television channels, newspapers and magazines worldwide, the amazing and intriguing world of Neopets now boasts multitudes of games, an awe-inspiring gaming world and an overwhelming interactive experience as you, the player, evolve your game play and grow alongside your pet as a person and friend. Welcome to the wonderful world of Neopets.

Project Neopets began as a small game created on a whim by Adam and Donna while they were in their college years. While Donna focused on the artwork and ideas, responsibility for programming and site work fell upon Adam's more than capable shoulders. The concept was simple. During the Tamagotchi era when virtual pets were on the rampage, Neopets provided an avenue for people to own a virtual pet on the Internet. A person would create his or her pet from a selection of many species, and then would be charged with feeding it, playing with it to keep it happy, and building a home to house their pet. To fund these activities, a person required a currency system, called Neopoints. Neopoints could be earned by playing games, gambling via the lottery and emulations of card games, and by opening a shop and selling items, which were obtained either by buying them or randomly finding them around the site.

In its first year alone, Neopets began drawing in thousands of people worldwide. Hardly focusing on advertising itself into culture through more direct means, the game was rapidly infiltrating mainstream society through word of mouth and recommendations by other players. The world had never seen such a thing. An easily accessible gaming experience which incorporated the best aspects of game classics, the interaction, the novelty, the many possible paths and specializations a person could choose and the never-ending challenge with no clear finish line were clear indications of Neopets' possibilities for success.

Incredibly, all this was free. Neopets was supported via a system of integrated advertisements, now more commonly referred to as product placement. Running by the slogan 'We'll always be free!' Neopets has kept true to its word, and has continued in its endeavor to provide each new player with the best possible experience that can be gained from such a game.

While it was not the original intention, Neopets, apart from being a totally engrossing past time, has significant education value. Not unlike other facets of real life, this game is riddled with puzzles of logic which tests the player's problem solving skills, is infiltrated with scammers who provide all players with a quick How-Not-To-Get-Scammed 101 lesson, and has provided avenues of gaming experiences, which quickly teach the player that gambling never prospers. In addi-

tion, its own system of a stock market exists for those wanting to learn how the trade works, while its option of having shops quickly teaches every user valuable and all-too-important commerce skills. With its currency system, everyone is able to learn valuable economic concepts, including how to budget carefully. Clearly, Neopets is a work of genius, and if its past growths are anything to go by, we can surely expect even better things to come.

Gathow
Artwork by Megan Cubbage

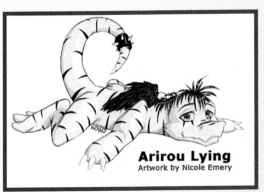

Arirou Lying
Artwork by Nicole Emery

Pojo Note: Did you know that in 1999, Neopets.com was one of the largest sponsors of Pojo.com? YEP! The folks at Neopets.com wanted to tap into our Pokemon fan base to help grow their site. Tens of thousands of people first discovered Neopets through Pojo.com!

Getting On

By: Kym Huynh

Neopets isn't a complicated world. However, one of the biggest things a player will have to adapt to is the sheer amount of information he or she will have to process in order to adequately begin playing the game. The game concept may be simple enough, but the changes, which constantly occur, are anything but simple. Because of this, the game can be darn right confusing. Our information in this section will help give you that competitive edge, making your gaming experience so much more fun as you leave your friends and adversaries eating your dust as you speed off into the horizon.

The Neopets Menu

The Neopets menu is divided into similar interest groups. These links will take you to areas most commonly accessed by players.

Pet Central

Pet Central is the area you go to automatically after you create your pet. It is sometimes seen as the center of your Neopet's interactive life. This is where you can check out what special abilities your pets may possess (abilities which are granted from freeing bottled faeries), view any trophies won in contests and games, visit your own neohome, or take a peek at all the extra resources which are available, such as computer desktop backgrounds, screensavers, buddy icons, fun images and shop blogs.

Add Pet

Here you can create a Neopet to add to your family. Initially when you create your account, you will be asked to create one pet. The maximum amount of Neopets you can have on one account is four. However, if you desire more than four Neopets, you are allowed to create them on separate accounts. Rare Neopets, although they do appear in the Add Pet option, are not creatable, and can only be gained by various other methods.

Neomail

This links to your mail inbox called Neomail. Here you can contact other Neopets players, and they can contact you back. This area also links you to your neofriends list, an area where you can keep track of all your friends

Aeri Human
Artwork by Megan Cubbage

on Neopets. Additionally, you can send anyone a neogreeting e-card or even record your journey with the neodiary!

World

Need to check the current Neopian time? This is where you should go! Also make sure to visit the world events listing, the gallery of evil, calendar and very fun how-to-draw pages for extra arts and craft fun!

Explore

No journey is complete unless you make a travel of some kind, and the Neopian worlds provide it easy for you and have created many worlds for you to explore! If you are in the mood to explore distant and exciting lands, then visit here first to get a complete listing of where you can go.

Chat

Want to interact with other Neopians? The NeoBoards allow you to chat in real time with people everywhere in the world! With practically every major topic on Neopets covered by the boards, this place is a great place to ask for help if you are stuck in a rut.

Leaping Mteke
Artwork by Megan Cubbage

Game Room

The following pages link you to all the games that can be played on Neopets, ranging from interactive multiplayer games to the Stock Market, and the flash Neopets games! As a major player in your initial neopoint income, the games room is a must for every player.

Objects

Linking to all the official shops, your inventory, the bank, notice board and other essentials, it is guaranteed that during your game play, you will visit this area at least once. It is the center of the commerce world in Neopets. If you're looking to create your shop, your bank account, or purchase any everyday items, this is your hot spot.

New Features

Need to keep on top of Neopets related news? Any new features, options or anything Neopets related will be reported here

Auvai
Artwork by Nicole Emery

by none other than the dedicated Neopets team, bringing you the latest in Neopets news 24/7!

Help

If you have any general questions and wouldn't mind an instant answer, then visit this area, as it will answer all your most common questions. Make sure you read this section when you first begin, as it will clear up many of those new player issues. Note however that the search function can only look up one word at a time.

Login / Logout

Click here to log in or log out. Essentially your key to entering the Neopian world, ensure that your password is not easily guessable and give it out to no one.

The User Lookup

Your User Lookup is a display of your achievements and an up-to-date account of your journey and travels. It allows other people to view your profile and it has an automatically updating badge, which will tell you by the month how long you have played Neopets. If you have also been fortunate enough to win contests and games, trophies will be proudly displayed here, with the exception of Neopet specific trophies such as the beauty contests. ●

The Neopets Toolbar

By: RedRocker

The Neopets Toolbar (which appears at the top of the screen when you enter Neopia Central, the Shop Wizard, and most other shop areas) is an essential tool for quickly navigating the Neopets site. Once you figure out how to effectively use this bar, you can get to all the essential locations much more

The Neopets Toolbar

From left to right, the icons are: Your Items, Your shop, Guild Head Quarters, Auction House, Shop Wizard, Notice Board, Battledome, The Bazaar, Main Shops, The Marketplace, Neopets Merchandise, Recent Price Changes, National Neopian Bank, Trading Post, Money Tree, and Safety Deposit Box.

Your Items

The colorful scoop of ice cream is the link to your inventory. This displays up to 50 items that you are carrying around. By clicking on the items in

your inventory and using the scroll-down menu, you can feed, groom, equip, read to, or play with your pet. Also using the scroll-down menu, you can stock things in your shop, store items in your Safety Deposit Box, put items up for trade, donate items, or discard them.

Your Shop

Clicking on the storefront will take you to the headquarters of your very own shop. Though it costs 150 Neopoints to first open the shop, and it can initially stock only five items, the investments of opening and upgrading are well met with profits. Once you start using the shop, money from sales can be withdrawn from the shop till.

Guild Head Quarters

The house icon will take you to the central spot for all guild members. Guilds are clubs

created by Neopians where those who share similar interests can talk, trade items, and organize nearly anything together. You can only be a member of one guild, whether it is one you create yourself or one you join. Note that some guilds are private, and you can only be accepted if the guild owner neomails you.

Auction House

With a gavel-shaped icon, the Neopian Auction House is a place where you can bid on items other people are auctioning off, or where you can auction off your own items. The auctions are open to all Neopians, and the highest bidder at the end of the set time limit gets the item. The transfer of Neopoints and items are automatic once the auction has ended, though it may take up to 24 hours for the transaction to take place. If you put an item up and no one bids on it, you will get the item back.

The Shop Wizard

The Shop Wizard's purple tent leads to the Neopets version of comparison shopping. The Wizard can search for any item you'd like, and will produce a list of private shops which have that item stocked, by lowest price. The Shop Wizard only searches a fraction

Puppyblew
Artwork by Megan Cubbage

of the private stores at a time though, so you may have to refresh the page a few times to find the absolute lowest price.

Notice Board

On the notice board, people pay to post their classified ads for guilds, shops, personal pet pages – virtually anything. The more you pay, the higher your ad goes on the board. This is an excellent place to advertise, if you have that kind of money to spare.

The Battledome

Clicking on the pink plushie will take you to the Battledome. In the Battledome, your pets can duke it out with other pets from all over Neopia. Two pets battle in a turn-based fashion, using learned attacks, abilities, and equipment to try to reduce the opponent's health to 0 before he or she does the same to you. In the Two-Player mode, you can challenge a friend (or enemy) if you know the name of their pet. In One Player mode, set challengers from the world will be available to fight, labeled with their difficulty level. It is recommended you don't fight the harder pets before your pet becomes a lot stronger.

The Bazaar

The left most part of the oval in the middle will take you to the Bazaar. Located directly next to Neopia Central, the Bazaar contains more shops, such as Pizzaroo, Usuki Land, Hubert's Hot Dogs, and the Chocolate Factory. Come here for deals on food, toys, collectable cards, and whatever else you can imagine!

Neopia Central Shops

The cheeseburger shaped icon, Neopia Central is home to all the necessary shops you need to raise your Neopet. The Neopian Bank, Food Shop, Book Shop, Hospital, and Pharmacy are among the buildings located here.

The Marketplace

The rightmost section of the oval, the Marketplace of Neopia Central is home to the top 500 private shops. The shops are organized by size, with the bigger shops at the top of the page. This is also the official home of the Shop Wizard.

Neopets Merchandise

Why limit your Neopet fun to the computer? This is the headquarters for real life Neopets merchandise. Here you can get news on new toy releases, as well as trade in any item codes you get from Neopets CCG cards.

Recent Price Changes

The bulletin board icon takes you to a listing of recent price changes Neopian shops have made. The prices are occasionally increased or reduced depending on the average price the Shop Wizard produces for the items.

National Neopian Bank

The closed safe leads to the Neopian Bank. Everyone has the opportunity to open a free bank account, where you can keep your Neopoints under lock and key while earning daily interest. The more money you have in your bank account, the higher the interest rate you have.

The Trading Post

Marked by a girl with a flower in her hair, the trading post is an outlet where Neopians can safely exchange items and Neopoints. People start lots

Jitei
Artwork by Katie Hartman

with all the items they would like to trade, and they make bargains with other players.

The Money Tree

The Money Tree is a place where people can donate Neopoints and items, and other players can pick them up. It's a great place to find free stuff, but be warned – there are consequences for being too greedy. Also, it's rumored that you will have good luck if you donate to the tree.

Safety Deposit Box

The open safe at the end of the toolbar is your safety deposit box. Every player is provided with a safe to store their items in. This is a great place to store things you don't want thieves to grab, and also a place where you can put items that won't fit in your inventory. The Box is totally safe, so don't be shy about depositing your items. ●

Neopian Lands

By Kym Huynh

In the world of Neopets there are many strange and exotic lands that can be explored at leisure by you. There are still many lands and locations which have not yet been discovered; however, be wary that many new areas have accompanying threats, which require the amassed efforts of every Neopian to save the world.

Lupe
Artwork by Megan Cubbage

Meridell

Meridell has a big history behind it. Discovered by a small band of children, this medieval country's issues shook the foundations of Neopia. An epic battle between Darigan and Meridell took place. The home of knights and damsels in distress, Meridell is famous for its brave deeds and epic tales of romance and adventure.

Krawk Island

Home of the Krawk Petpets, this island was the original haven for pirates where treasure was buried and mischief ran amok. For those who love a life of excitement and adventure, this island, located southwest of Mystery Island, is the place to go. It is rumored that treasures from the past are still hidden somewhere beneath the sand.

The Lost Desert

The land where Brucey B and his legions fought into lore and legend, the Lost Desert came about during the second major epic war between good and evil. If you have a great love of sand and the mystery behind the pyramid formations, make sure your Neopet is blessed with spells before venturing forth into the unknown sands.

Tyrannia

The land of prehistoric dinosaurs and ancient beings, Tyrannia exists on vast amounts of dry rock, in an area many miles below the Ice Cave. The Tyrannian Plateau contains a Giant Omelette that will provide food for your Neopets once a day for free if you visit.

Faerieland

Home of the faeries and the legendary Faerie Queen herself, this land is only accessible through flying thousands of feet skywards. Located directly above Neopian Central, Faerieland is also the home for the elusive Hidden Tower, which houses some of the most powerful (and expensive) items and equipment in all of Neopia.

Terror Mountain

Don't let the name scare you. This land is covered in ice, which make it an ideal skating park! At the base of this mountain lies Happy Valley, the most sought after holiday destination during Christmas and winter seasons and celebrations. Further up the mountains are the Ice Caves, famous for the Snowager, who jealously guards a hefty amount of treasure. At the top of the mountain lies the Ski Lodge. Rumor has it that a big mystery occurred there a few years back. What was it? Nobody knows...

Mystery Island

Mystery it is indeed. It is home to the Cooking Pot Faerie, Jhudiah. Mystery Island is also the home to the Trading Post, where Neopians can safely trade goods and Neopoints with other Neopians. If you visit, be prepared to lie on the beach, kick back and relax!

Virtupets Space Station

The original base of Dr. Sloth, this Space Station was converted into an amusement arcade after Dr. Sloth's original plan to transform every pet into a mutant was foiled by the efforts of many Neopians. It is also where the heroic deeds of the Space Faerie could be witnessed as she fought for the existence of Neopia. Although she won, she was exhausted after the battle with Dr. Sloth, and ever since, there have only been small sightings of the Space Faerie.

Haunted Woods

Often described as scary and thrilling, this spooky world is home to chilling calls and hoots. Be wary that the Brain Tree doesn't catch you, for the consequences of not answering his questions are said to be great. Make sure you visit the Deserted Fairground! ●

Neopets

By Kym Huynh

Did You Know

That the Aisha started its life with a kite attached to its tail, but the kite was removed at the last minute before the Aisha was made public.

The complete guide to all of the Neopets, the following pages contain vital statistics and fun facts for all those Neopets junkies out there! Including descriptions and special abilities, each Neopet species is explored to leave you with an intuitive decision on what will work and what will leave you disappointed. With instructions on how to discover the rarest Neopets in existence, you can't go wrong with this chapter!

this ability to give hope to anyone is perhaps the most powerful ability of all.

Aisha

Undoubtedly the most intelligent of all Neopets species, some even claim this Neopet possesses a certain degree of psychic power. Whether this means the ability to read minds or move objects with their mind (telekinetic powers) remains to be seen; however, what is certain is their amazing scientific and technological ingenuity. Believed to have moved to Neopia after a tragic accident on their home planet, there have been claims that some have discovered and unearthed the alien spaceships Aisha ancestors used to mass migrate to Neopia. If you do adopt an Aisha, be sure to provide it with many books to read, as nothing makes them happier.

Blumaroo

High on sugar and bouncy – who could ask for a more fun companion? Known for being extremely silly and thinking up ludicrous ideas, this Neopet is perfect for those who don't mind bouncing to and from places. This Neopet is joyous to have around, and its ever-optimistic nature will always put a smile on your face!

Bruce

Cute and cuddly are two words that spring to mind when thinking about this

pet. Joyful in nature and in life, Bruces love competition, and if you place a Bruce near other Neopets, you will soon see them running around trees, running around houses in an attempt to see who is faster. Bruces excel at ice-skating, so much that there have been games created featured on this single aspect!

Buzz

Extremely fast and energetic, this hardy Neopet uses its four wings to gain extreme momentum and speed very quickly. While it may look somewhat fierce, this Neopet will be content if given fruits and berries to nibble on and is quite friendly. Woe

Striped Acara
Artwork by Krista Nicholson

Acara

With those cute eyes, cute ears, and cute looks, how could a person not help but fall in love with these cute creatures? Their wide-eyed innocence, trusting nature and giggles have the ability to charm a bird off its branch. A perfect addition to any family, this Neopet will always bring joy and hope, even during times when there seems to be no light. Perhaps it is their innocence that creates this, but

Sako
Artwork by Megan Cubbage

beholds any who dare attempt to hurt it or its friends, however, as its lightning fast reflexes will shock the attacker before he or she can even think of running away.

Chia

The first Neopet to ever reveal itself, the Chia is a very interesting creature. Its strange genetic makeup renders the Chia in a constant state of change, exemplified when a Chia eats certain foods. Initially, people were alarmed that a Chia would turn into a pineapple after eating a pineapple, however now that people have come to realize the nature of the mysterious Chia, it is not uncommon to see Chias shaped like apples, lemons and limes walking up and down the walkways in Neopia. Extremely friendly and caring, expect a hug from this creature if you meet one.

Chomby

An herbivore, this prehistoric Neopet's long neck enables it to reach to the tops of trees where the green leaves are juiciest. While it is quite shy, this Neopet's huge size and hard skin make it a formidable opponent in the Battledome. One of the greatest joys of raising a Chomby is watching it in its early years, as they are quite clumsy!

Curious Chomby
Artwork by Krista Nicholson

Cybunny

Sporting a lion-like mane, these carrot munchers can survive in Neopia's coldest regions because their thick fur is able to keep them warm even in extreme conditions. A great addition to any family, the Cybunny is often confused with the Easter Bunny, who looks a great deal similar. Watch out for the Cybunny's legs, as they can pack a very powerful kick!

Draik

These Neopets are rumored to have originated from another world. One sunny day during Neopia's warmer months, a flock of Draiks was seen flying through the sky. To the amazement of Neopians below, these dragon-like creatures were very cute and friendly, and their ability to fly made traveling to Faerieland a great deal easier!

Elephante

While enormous in size, the Elephante is surprisingly quick and nimble. Its docile nature enables it to get along with anyone easily. Its calm exterior belies a potent weapon, its trunk, which is capable of firing any item very accurately in a missile-like fashion. Its small wings are also very powerful, capable of lifting the Elephante off the ground, although the Elephante is limited to hovering.

Eyrie

Considerably intelligent, this Neopet will never give up the opportunity to debate any topics that it deems intelligent and stimulating. Linked to the mythical griffins, these Neopets have powerful beaks that pack a nasty bite if anyone is unwise enough to

Sankura
Artwork by Megan Cubbage

annoy them. Also blessed with the ability to fly, this Neopet is seen as many as a utility Neopet. It can be a handy Neopet to have around when that book on the bookshelf is a little out of reach!

Flotsam

Dolphin-like joy and sleek, this water bound Neopet is rumored to be one of the fastest swimmers in existence. Flotsams love racing the ocean waves, and often people visit the Neopian coast just to marvel at their antics.

Gelert

Distant cousins to the Lupe, Gelerts are the embodiment of all that is fun and goofy. They are joyous creatures with a love of anyone and everything. If you are exhausted from a long day at work, there is nothing better than coming home to a Gelert, who will do anything possible to make your day a happier day. Legend and myth have been written about their brave deeds. Such stories have made the Gelert a household name. If anything, their love of children makes them excellent baby sitters. However, don't let their fun-loving nature fool you: like their Lupe cousins, they're fiercely protective of their friends and family.

Grarrl

Strong and proud, the Grarrl is a fierce Neopet that should only be handled by people who are experienced with raising Neopets. Short tempered and very powerful, this Neopet will go on a rampage when angered, and won't stop for several hours. Able to eat anything and everything in its path, the Grarrl's sharp claws and teeth make it an unrivaled and potent fighter with excellent attack power. Approach these Neopets with caution, and run if you find one in a rampage!

Grundo

Grundos were once imprisoned by Dr. Sloth's evil regime. Through his evil ways and experiments, he mutated the peace loving Grundo into beefed up, mind-warped warriors. Only through the collaborative efforts of all the citizens of Neopia and the Space Faerie were the Grundos freed from their cruel enslavement and adopted into new caring homes. Grundos, like Aishas, are believed to have come to Neopia from space. While their cute demeanor may be a bit on the goofy side, their intelligence should not be underestimated.

Ixi

The Ixi are hardy forest and wood creatures that are renowned for their cunning and intelligence. Their speed is also something to be marveled at as watching them leap and bound through the forest is a sight to see. Initially they may appear shy, but they are always willing to lend a hand should anything go wrong. If you enter

their habitat with bad intentions, be forewarned that they are the masters of the wood, and will not tolerate such ill intentions.

Jetsam

Cousins to the Flotsam, the Jetsam are the gangsters of the sea. While many view them as the pirates of the Caribbean, many epics and tales have portrayed these Neopets as misunderstood souls who crave for someone to care for them. Whether this is true or not, it is certain that those who have befriended these creatures have made a powerful ally, and their days are now filled with excitement and adventure.

JubJub

JubJubs are adorably cute and cuddly. While it may look like a big ball of fluff with two legs, those legs can pack a nasty kick when provoked. Often recommended as a companion for children, this Neopet loves being hugged and played with, so adopting another one to keep it company is never a bad decision!

Kacheek

Shy and peaceful, Kacheeks are often seen bouncing and prancing

Mteke
Artwork by Megan Cubbage

Yellow Grundo
Artwork by Krista Nicholson

Ixi Faerie
Artwork by Katie Hartman

though. They'll never give up a chance for some fun, and their mischievous grins are incurably infectious. Unfortunately, a mysterious disaster ruined their native city Maraqua, and all that remains are ruins. Most Kois are currently homeless, so Neopian citizens have been adopting these Neopets like crazy. Their help around the house is invaluable.

around Neopian meadows. Their bright colorings enable them to quickly hide amongst the flowers and trees and their fun-loving nature is a wonder to behold.

Kau

The Kau's milk has restorative powers. Gentle and peace loving, Kaus love large green pastures on which they can feed. In battle, the Kau's focus is more defensive than offensive, but that doesn't mean it can't still pack a punch. Its horns are sharp enough to teach those who annoy it a lesson they won't forget. Kaus are natural mothers, and should you want to search for one, look no further than a hospital or community orientated project. Also extremely intelligent, Kaus are known for their magical potion-making ingenuity.

Kiko

This strange amphibian Neopet, while nearly always appearing in water, has the ability to travel across land. It also appears to sport a bandage on its head. The purpose of this bandage is unknown. Kikos can pack mean water pumped attacks on anything they view as a potential threat.

Koi

Excellent mechanical engineers and inventors, nearly anything you find in Neopia was invented by these clever fish related Neopets. That's not just to say these Neopets are all brains

Did You Know

Koi is the Japanese word for carp.

Kougra

Originating from Mystery Island, this Neopet's cute and playful nature combined with its large paws and pointy teeth make it a natural in the Battledome. These cheeky buggers love to pounce on unsuspecting playmates, so if you plan to introduce this Neopet to your family and friends, make sure that its playmate does not confuse the Kougra's playfulness for aggression.

Korbat

Seen flying and gliding around Neopia during the night rather than the day, these friendly creatures are great lovers of fruit and berries. They love these fruits so much that they are

often seen swooping around Meridell farmland in search of these berries. If you are fortunate enough to own a Korbat, you'll always be guaranteed a full basket of fruit at home.

Krawk

The Krawk is the only species in existence that is a petpet mutation. One day, an owner took his Neopet to a cave filled with glowing fungus. The Neopet in question also brought along his petpet, which was incidentally a Krawk. When the petpet ate the fungus, it slowly mutated into a full-grown Krawk. Classified by scientists as a Neopet and a petpet, this creature loves mischief and it is a common sight to see a shop keeper chase a Krawk down the street while the Krawk runs away with a string of sausages, laughing gleefully. Also a seasoned fighter, this Neopet's outgoing nature and natural fighting ability make it a prime candidate for Battledome veterans.

How to Find a Krawk

Ensure you do not have more than three Neopets on your account, as

Kopuyo
Artwork by Megan Cubbage

you will require an additional space to add a Krawk Neopet. Equip your active Neopet with a Krawk Petpet, and then visit the Fungus Cave located on Krawk Island. Have your Krawk Petpet eat the glowing fungus and watch it mutate into a fully-grown Krawk!

Kyrii

Gregarious and extremely friendly, these Neopets are often seen in groups of 3 or more. Intelligent and full of life, Kyriis are recommended as a perfect addition to any family as they're naturally caring and will go out of their way to make sure that everyone around them is as comfortable as they can be. Sometimes their friendliness can go a little too far, and they may prefer being a friend to their brothers and sisters rather than being a brother or sister themselves.

Lenny

One of the least seen Neopets, the Lenny is naturally tall and overtly cheerful yet highly intelligent. Its strut can only be described as graceful in a clumsy way, yet this species high degree of intelligence and quick thinking make it one of the prime candidates for enrollment in Battledome strategy and magic energy use and distortion. The Lenny posses a powerful inner knowledge, which only reveals itself in times of need.

Did You Know

The amount of letters in your Neopet's name will determine some of its dislikes. For example, if your pet's name contains five letters, your Neopet will refuse to have anything to do with any other item that also contains five letters.

Lupe

These Neopets are loyal steadfast and protective of their owners, friends, and families. Once you have befriended a Lupe, expect a friend for life! With four strong legs and a bite to match, this Neopet is one of the bravest, and will help protect its brothers and sisters in hostile situations. This species has played a large part in Neopian history. Jeran, a legendary Lupe character that played a very large part in the Meridell and Darigan wars, was an advisor to King Skrarll.

Meerca

Famous for its long, strong tail, the Meerca can be seen scampering up and down Neopian homes, forests and woods. Extremely quirky and cheeky, these Neopets are natural jokers and will play pranks on unsuspecting people and pets. While they may be one of the smaller species, their speed and wit more than makes up for what they lack in size.

Moehog

Initially considered a very rare Neopet, this creature has starting appearing around Neopia more frequently. Considered by many as a rebel with a cause, this Neopet is often seen in the middle of concerts partying with the best of them.

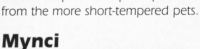

Moofeathers
Artwork by Katie Hartman

Perhaps the music from the growing population attracted these music-loving creatures. Whatever the cause, this pet's fun loving attitude, street smarts and humor make it a prime candidate for any family. Just make sure to keep this Neopet separated from the more short-tempered pets.

Mynci

Mynci, the monkey Neopet is what would be described as an all-rounder. Cute yet strong, cheeky yet loyal, this Neopet's innate sense of loyalty and balance ensures that it is often seen around Neopia performing various feats and tasks, from shopping to helping their owners build a new stall or house. These Neopets are among the more versatile species, as their fingered hands and arm-like tail can grasp and hold onto objects in a similar fashion to humans.

Lab Pet Love
Artwork by Katie Hartman

Nimmo

These Neopets are often thought of as the masters of meditation and the epitome of good virtue. Living on the belief that their faith will protect them, these Neopets' high spirituality renders it a very loyal and steadfast friend.

Peophin

Considered one of the most stunning and beautiful Neopets, the Peophin is a seaborne Neopet that is considered by many one of the most dazzling yet mysterious Neopets in existence. Citizens of Neopia one day noticed sleek and graceful movements in the clear waters off the coast of Neopia Central, but where they originated from is unknown.

Poogle

Originating from Northern Neopia, these Neopets have the potential to pack quite a wallop in the Battledome, as their cute exterior hides extremely sharp teeth. Naturally, these Neopets are quite good natured, and considerate, how-ever it is advised to back away if Poogle ears lower and they start to freeze up. One will be able to tell if a Poogle is friendly is by the wagging of their tails.

Pteri

The only bird-like Neopet with exceptional flying ability is the Pteri. Somewhat cheeky in nature, these Neopets sometimes share their treetop homes with the scampering Meercas, and it is not an uncommon sight to see these two Neopets at it together tricking passersby with their clever tricks and jokes. Pteris originate from Tyrannia, and living in such a tough and hardy neighborhood has evolved

Did You Know

The Shoyru is the only Neopet that was created by a Neopian player.

them into extremely fast navigators of the sky.

Quiggle

These frog-like amphibians love eating flies, and anything else people might consider yucky! They are often found sun-baking on rocks and hopping and skipping among the ponds and lakes they reside at. Quiggles can ribbit with the best of them. If you find your NeoHome invaded by thousands of insects, asking a few of your Quiggle friends to hop along to your house will clean up the small problem in no time!

Scorchio

These Neopets are extremely friendly and will never turn down an offer for adventure and excitement! If you ever decide to travel and explore the Neopian Mountains, don't be surprised to see some Scorchios scaling the rocky cliffs with ease. Their enthusiasm for fun and mischief is catching, so if you and your Neopets ever need a great pick-me-up, befriend a Scorchio. Their fiery origin will ensure an exciting family life.

Shoyru

Need a quick method to travel to the far and distant lands of Neopia? Fancy a winter holiday up in Snow Valley or to visit the home of the faeries in Faerieland? Shoyrus possess powerful wings which can fly you there before you can say 'holiday'. Shy by nature, this dragonish Neopet is very versatile and is a ferocious fighter, making this pet a prime candidate for people who visit the Battledome.

Skeith

These Neopets will eat anything! One of the biggest Neopets, this pet is renowned for its great defense and attack power, which can be attributed to its colossal size. Unfortunately, what it possesses in attack and defense power it lacks in speed. In the history of Neopets, never has a Skeith been known to win a race. Their habit of eating anything it can carry is also somewhat worrying. It's rough outside nature may also convey the message of unfriendliness, but once this Neopet is yours, you'll have an environmentally friendly living garbage disposal unit on your hands!

Techo

Unquestionably one of the happiest Neopets ever, Techos are a ray of light to any Neopet it encounters. Blessed with exceptional acrobatic skills, these natural performers are the life of any party and can hold any audience in tears of laughter for hours on end.

Tonu

Discovered in the mountains and valleys of Tyrannia, this Neopet is completely covered by a thick coat of skin, which will render any attack on it futile. Strong and powerful, this Neopet can handle and carry heavy loads with ease and is often seen helping out at construction sites. An exceptional fighter, this Neopets' rampaging charge is earth shattering. When a Tonu charges, get out of the way!

How to Find a Tonu

New Tonus only make periodic appearances into the Neopets population, and when they do, there will be a mad rush to befriend them. Numbers are limited and their appearances are random, so the best method to finding out when they appear is to keep tabs in the Neopets Chat Boards for notices other Neopian citizens leave! If you are lucky enough to find one, enter the Create-A-Pet page quickly and grab one before they're all taken!

Tuskaninny

Seal-like, this Neopet has huge teeth and an insatiable love of fish. It is easily found near the icy waters of Terror Mountain and Snow Valley. Offer this Neopet a fish and it'll be more than happy to follow you around for the

Red Scorchio
Artwork by Krista Nicholson

day. More interested in playing than fighting, you'll be hard pressed to find a Tuskaninny near any Battledome arena. Woe befalls anyone who comes between a Tuskaninny and its fish. Perhaps that is the secret to unleashing their real power.

Uni

The most beautiful and vainest Neopet in existence, this Neopet's beauty is unrivaled. Unis will spend hours brushing their flowing manes and stare endlessly at their reflections every time they pass a mirror. Supply this Neopet with a good supply of assorted brushes and beauty accessories to keep it extremely happy. Be warned, however: should you ever go shopping with this Neopet by your side, make sure you carry a thick wad of cash, as the Uni has very expensive tastes in designer clothes and accessories.

Usul

Naturally caring, this Neopet will always ensure that its company is comfortable before paying attention

to itself. Extremely loyal and giving, Usuls are examples of everything that is good and true in this world. Living on the belief that, "to be loved, one must love," these Neopets are always welcome to any family.

Wocky

Like the Scorchio, the Wocky is extremely outgoing, friendly and adventurous. Wockys love the great outdoors and the feel of the wind on a sailing ship out on the seas; therefore these Neopets are often the discoverers of treasure. Unafraid and brave, the Wocky is a perfect and powerful member of any battling adventurer.

Zafara

Zafaras are the bringers of good will and good luck to anyone who treats them with respect, love and friendship. If you know any friends that have won the lottery recently or have stumbled upon a rare treasure, check to see if they have any Zafaras! ●

Care and Feeding

By Kym Huynh

Like sunlight is to a tree, food is necessary for Neopets (unless you like to see your Neopet described as starving -bad!). Part of the duties you have as an owner, is to make sure your Neopets are well fed and looked after. However, did you also know that certain Neopets have certain special effects from eating various types of food? For instance, no matter how hungry your Kau may be, if it eats any milk related product, it will instantly fill itself full.

f not properly cared for and neglected, Neopets can get sick, ranging from flu-like symptoms to more serious illnesses such as the neopox. Additionally, what you feed your Neopet should be carefully monitored, as some Neopets are allergic to certain types of foods.

You can tell if a Neopet is sick by looking at its quick reference page (the page where you can change your active pet) or the pet's search information page. They will either appear wrapped in bandages and looking forlorn as they wait for you to provide them with medical attention. ●

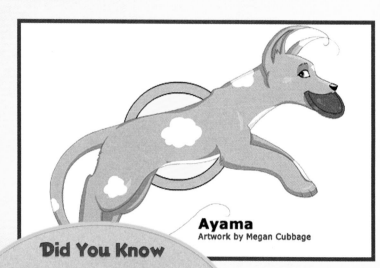

Ayama
Artwork by Megan Cubbage

Did You Know

If fed ice cream, Quiggles will become sick. Because Quiggles are amphibians, they spend most of the day in the sun warming up. Eating ice cream makes them cold again.

Did You Know

The Water Faerie in Faerieland can sometimes heal your sick Neopets for free. Simply visit her every so often and sometimes, she will magically cure them of any illness they have, fill up their stomachs, or increase their hit points temporarily!

Baby Uni
Artwork by Kismet

Adoptions

By Kym Huynh

Unfortunately, sometimes people discover that they cannot handle taking care of more than one pet. Many of the abandoned Neopets can be found at the Adoption Center. For those with large hearts, they are given the option of adopting the abandoned Neopets to feed and care for them as their own.

If you chose to adopt a pet, remember that the pet name cannot be changed. This may be an issue to some people, as some owners like to give Neopets very random and not very nice names. However, as William Shakespeare once wrote in his much-acclaimed play Romeo and Juliet, 'A rose by any other name would smell as sweet' – It is not the name that matters but the heart behind the Neopet.

Adopting Neopets will also incur a small charge, which is the cover cost for taking care of the Neopet when it was in the pound. The stronger and more powerful the Neopet is, the higher the cost will be to adopt it. The charges are relatively small, so this shouldn't be too much of an issue.

If you do decide to adopt a Neopet, visit the adoption center in Pet Central and inform reception of your intentions. You will then be shown random Neopets from which you can choose one.

The Pounding Debate

Many arguments have been thrown back and forth surrounding the contentious issues of pounding or essentially, 'giving up' a Neopet. Some claim that there are already too many aban-

White Aisha
Artwork by Krista Nicholson

Koko Loves Arirou
Artwork by Nicole Emery

doned Neopets in the pound, and to subject the Neopet to the pound is cruel and unnecessary. On the other hand, some asserted that sometimes, a person must be cruel to be kind. People who advocate such views have expressed that it is better the Neopet be placed in the pound to find a better person who can take care of them, as the current owner is unable or unwilling to adequately take care of them. What are your views?

I'm a firm believer of giving the Neopet to a better owner if for some reason you find that you cannot take care of your Neopet anymore, but more recently, there has also been a method of passing your Neopet off to a different owner, without the need to leave it in the pound for extended periods of time. This method is called 'transferring pets'.

Transferring Neopets

Should a player decide to transfer their Neopet, whether to another account or to a friend, using the pound to send Neopets has become a common practice. There are dangers of course, but hopefully the method shown below will make the process as quick and as efficient as possible.

This method will require two people. One person will need to be logged into the account with the Neopet that they want to be transferred. The other person needs to be logged into the second account, which they want to receive the pet. If your person helping you is accessing one of your accounts, make sure this is a person you can trust and not some random person off the NeoBoards, who once in your account, will run off with anything valuable

Burglar Kougra
Artwork by Krista Nicholson

quicker than you can exclaim, "what the?!?"

Have both people visit the Neopian Pound. The person on the receiving end should visit the 'Adopt-A-Pet' area and in the search field, type in the Neopet's name. The other person in

the other account also needs to visit the Neopian Pound. However, this person will need to go to the abandon option. As soon as one person abandons the pet into the pound, the other person needs to be notified immediately, whereby they can load up the adoption pages and adopt the pet pronto!

Because there are many players in the adoption pounds, transferring rare pets should be done carefully. Therefore, it is recommended that the two people are able to keep in contact via online messaging clients.

Important Note

Make sure the receiving account does not already have four Neopets. If it does, it will be unable to grab the recently abandoned Neopet.

Oh no! Someone else adopted the Neopet before I could transfer it!

In the worst-case scenario, the pet you were attempting to transfer, or

receive was snatched up by another person who was visiting the pound. In this case, you can find out who adopted your Neopet by running a name search in Neopets' search directory. The new owner's name will show up on the Neopet's owner description.

By neomailing the new owner, politely explain what happened and request that the Neopet be placed back in the pound for you to receive. Be careful however as the new owner is under no obligation to place the Neopet back in the pound for you and may keep it if he or she wishes. In addition, DO NOT offer Neopoints in return for the Neopet as the local Neopian authority will freeze you in your tracks faster than you can say, "I didn't do it."

Before transferring a pet via the pound, be aware of the risks involved and if you do decide to go ahead with transferring, be prepared to accept the consequences that it is possible that the wrong person could snatch up the pet. ●

Neopoints

By Kym Huynh

Neopoints is the currency system in Neopia. Using Neopoints, a person can buy items, stock from the stock market, bid in auctions, and trade for other items on Neopets. While the prices of individual items vary, the trading, which occurs within shops and auctions, are what keeps the economy alive and well.

How Do I Get Them?

Neopoints can be gained from many different activities. Initially, players will make most of their income from playing games on Neopets. The higher a person scores, the greater the point returns.

After a small amount of Neopoints has been saved up, players have various options. They can either choose to spend it all on more items, or they can choose to invest it in the banking system, which give interests returns every day for keeping the money in the bank! For budding business enthusiasts, there is also an option to open a store, which allows the user to resell items they gain either from finding or

buying them. There are many other forms of neopoint gaining activities, which will be explored below.

Getting Neopoints through Games

Gaining Neopoints through games is one of the first ways players can earn Neopoints. Gaming enthusiasts will find this an essential source of income day after day. Generally, Neopets provides every user with access to games with differing difficulty ratings. Typically, the harder a game is, the greater the neopoint returns. Many Neopians who play by this method choose two or three games to specialize in. They play those games repeatedly until they know every trick and secret. Using this information, they start achieving awesome scores, and may possibly end up on the high score table. The higher the score is, the more Neopoints they get. Also, if they end up on the high score table, they win a trophy for their achievements, and get a prize return every night of that month. Theoretically, if a player masters all the games, he/she could be drawing in 100,000+ Neopoints a day! As Neopets allows a person to receive neopoint returns three times a day per individual game, the Neopoints can add up

very quickly! This method however is very time-consuming, and not recommended to people who want to see the Neopoints quickly.

Getting Neopoints through Opening a Store

This is often cited as the best method of gaining Neopoints. When a user chooses to open a shop, he or she pays a small deposit to reserve a piece of land for the shop. Initially, the shop can only hold five items to sell, but the shop is able to be permanently upgraded, five item slots at a time. Some users have even upgraded their shop into large convenience stores, boasting shop sizes of 200+ units, which enable the user to stock their shop with thousands of items!

A user stocks his or her shop by either finding or buying items in other

Robot Spalix
Artwork by Katie Hartman

shops. Users gain Neopoints by reselling these items. The official Neopets shops are often inundated with other players, waiting for the shops to stock, so they can quickly grab items to stock their own stores. The official Neopets Stores are notoriously known for underpricing items which players are willing to pay thousands for! A player who chooses this method of playing, however, requires a very fast internet connection (cable or faster), and the knowledge of which items are the best to buy.

Essentially, players who play this method are called 'restockers'. Haggling skills are not important here, as you are attempting to grab the item before another player does. 'Restocking' is a very popular method and used by the majority of players, as it enables new players to effectively become rich overnight!

Did You Know

Players have been pleasantly surprised to find that their stock values have increased by 500% in some instances if they were held for over a year. However, holding stocks for this long also poses a considerable risk, as companies behind the stocks have been known to periodically become bankrupt.

Neopets shops also stocks items that can be resold for millions, so keep a good look out for them if you decide to become a storeowner!

How to Effectively Set Your Prices

Buying an expensive item in the official stores is all well and good, but there is no point if you cannot sell the item. When selling through your own private store, you are competing with every other private storeowner out there, so you'll need to price your products accordingly so the public is encouraged to buy your product first.

Visit the Shop Wizard in Neopia Central. He will produce a list of prices among privately owned shops, from the lowest price up, for the item you input in his search feature. For more specific details, read the subsection "Shop Wizard" under Shopping.

Getting Neopoints through Investing

Only people who have built up a considerable sum of Neopoints should only use this method. With countless millions in their pocket, they simply deposit all their Neopoints in the Neopian bank and retrieve their daily interest from their sum to use for whatever they want. Because their initial deposit is so large, their interest returns are also considerable. Also, using the bank is free! Most restockers who have made it big have resorted to this method, as it is similar to the restocking and game playing method, except the hard work has initially been done, and now all they need to do is sit back and enjoy the ride!

Getting Neopoints through Auctions

A cousin to the restocking method, a user will prowl through the auctions, searching for the best deals. For some strange reason, items in the auctions tend to be under priced, so a user can easily bid on items, win auctions and then resell that item for a higher price in their stores!

Auctioneers should exercise caution when bidding, as they could be bidding on an item, which is overpriced. Bidding can become quite competitive, so people who plan to play with this method should polish up their auctioning skills! Most auctions are won within the last few seconds, so having a fast internet connection is a big help.

Getting Neopoints through Trading

Also a method where a good base of Neopoints is recommended, this strategy is best suited to players who know his or her items should only play this method, as the potential to lose a lot of Neopoints on this venture is very real and very possible.

If a player is smart and knows his or her items, he/she could easily trade items that are worth millions, for items they own which can be worth less, thereby making a gain of the difference between item one and item two. Traders who can sense when a player needs an item urgent, can up the prices for their items, safe with the knowledge that their items will be sold!

This method of playing is very similar to 'restocking'; however, the time in which an item is gained and sold is considerably longer. Many players like to combine the restocking method and the trading method to help bolster their potential gains quicker.

WARNING:

When you place an item you own on the trading post, some people like to bid 1 neopoint on your items. As Neopets provides an option to accept or reject an offer, many would assume this would not be a problem. However, it is not uncommon for a person to accidentally click accept, effectively selling their item worth millions for one neopoint. Once accept or deny is clicked, it cannot be reversed, so be very careful when someone bids on your lot. ●

RedRocker Tip:
Don't hold strictly to the idea that Neopets.com will restock their shops exactly every eight minutes. Some stores tend to restock regularly, while others may take ten to fifteen minutes to restock. If you decide to visit one shop in particular repeatedly, you can learn the restocking patterns in just a few days.

Shopping

By Kym Huynh

Shopping is an activity which Neopians practice to purchase their Neopet stoys, food and various other items. Many people also use this option to stock their own stores so they can resell their bought items. Unless you don´ tmind watching your Neopoints unnecessarily spill down the drain, learning haggling and shopping skills is a must´ at official shops anyway.

Shop Restocking

O ften when a Neopian visits official stores, they will find that the store is empty of items. This is usually because the store items were so popular, that they were cleaned out (the book shop is a classic example of this)! Neopets shops usually restock their items every eight minutes, so stick around and you'll have a chance of being one of the first people with first pick of items when they do restock. Just ensure you buy the items quickly before anyone else can!

Haggling

Haggling is the art of effectively bringing down the price of an item before paying for it. The shopkeepers never expect people to buy items for the price they advertise the items at and nor should you! They set higher prices, expecting that you will try to bargain it down by a few hundred to a few thousand depending on how much the initial price is.

When haggling, make an initial bid of half the price. Every time, make increments of 100 Neopoints or a fraction of the remaining asking price until both customer and shopkeeper are happy. Remember that the shopkeeper will always pretend to act outraged at your 'ridiculous' offers, however this is just an act to make you offer more! Be forewarned, if you waste too much of the shopkeepers time, they'll simply refuse to sell you the item and during

RedRocker Tip:
New shop owners may notice that if they use the Shop Wizard to price their items, the results come up different when they hit refresh. This is because the Shop Wizard searches a different chunk of shops every time. Wonder why you have a hard time finding your name, even if you price your items dirt cheap? The Shop Wizard doesn't order shops by shop size, popularity, or anything like that. It orders them alphabetically by the first letter of your user name. If you want to find where your shop would show up, you have to refresh the results until you find the list where the letter of your user name fits. That's the only way to get accurate prices.

The different letter groups are as follows:
a i q y 1 9
b j r z 2
c k s 3
d l t 4
e m u 5
f n v 6
g o w _ 7
h p x 0 8

this time, someone else may have bought the item you wanted!

The Shop Wizard

The shop wizard is an invaluable resource which is free to use and is accessible by all Neopians. The brain behind this ingenuity is the magical JubJub, who is able to search all privately owned stores for any item you ask. After the searches, it will return with a complete list of the least expensive prices currently set for that item.

What to Watch Out For

When you are buying items, be wary that you are not buying items that are overpriced. This caution is emphasized because in various shops, especially in the battle and defense shops, items tend to be sold overpriced. A better option is to buy them in privately owned shops. A good indication if an item is overpriced is the time it takes for it to go out of stock. Items which disappear quickly are under-priced items, which everyone wants!

Often, rare items and items which are under-priced are highly sought after by Neopians, as they can be resold in private stores for a handy little profit. If you are lucky enough to find these items, it might not be a bad idea to skip haggling for the item, and

buy it for the asking price before another Neopian grabs the item.

Shop Related - How to Price Items

Once you have opened a private shop and stocked it with items you wish to sell, your next task is to sell the items. If priced correctly, most items will sell out within twenty-four hours.

To ensure that an item is sold, send the shop wizard on a search for price of items you are selling. Once he comes back with the relevant information, price your item one neopoint below the lowest price. This encourages people to visit your shop over other shops!

How to Build a Shop

To build a shop, enter the shopping area in Neopets, and then apply to open a private store by clicking on the shop menu icon on the quick links bar near the top of the page. Once there, you will be asked if you will accept

the start-up fee. If you accept, click yes and you'll have your shop!

Why a Shop Should be Built

Considered one of the best ways to gain Neopoints, shops allow Neopians to sell and resell their items so they can make a handy little profit. Most people who utilize the shops are 'restockers' – people who purchase under priced items from the official Neopian stores and resell them in their own stores at a higher price. ●

Darigan Eyrie
Artwork by Kismet

Paint Brushes

By Kym Huynh

One of the coolest aspects of Neopets is the ability to dab your Neopet with a paintbrush, and watch it change colors and possibly shape right in front of you! As Neopets are able to be painted in various colors and shades, the options are unlimited there! The paintbrushes will allow Neopets to be painted according to themes, such as pirate and fire, while some paintbrushes can totally change the pets appearance! Have you ever wanted a faerie Neopet? It is possible with the Faerie Paint Brush!

Unfortunately, paintbrushes are very expensive. Even for a simple color change, Neopians are looking into hundreds of thousands. If people are lucky, the Paint Brush Phantom, who gives free paintbrushes to those it visits, can sometimes visit, however this is quite rare.

One of the most interesting paint brushes in existence is the Baby Paint Brush, which when used on your Neopet, will revert it back to its baby state. ●

Did You Know

Color isn't the only thing you can change about your Neopet. If it tickles your fancy, they can be turned into other species as well. Giving your Neopets a magical toy plushie or a magical potion is just some of the ways in which you can change your Neopets species.

Dragonsheir Ball
Artwork by Katie Hartman

Faeries of Neopia

By Kym Huynh

Special Faeries

Faerie Queen

Ruler of all faeries in Neopia, the Faerie Queen resides in the fluffy and cute world of Faerieland. She leads the crusade against dark and evil. In times of great need, this powerful faerie has been known to send various people powerful items to aid them in battle.

The Faerie Queen also sells powerful items enchanted with potent magic and enchantments to those who can find the secret Hidden Tower and to those who can afford the very expensive items.

Illusen

Residing in Meridell, this earth-based faerie is the twin sister to Jhudora, the dark faerie. For reasons unknown, these two had a falling out, and even then, it is still uncertain if the fight was staged for an ulterior motive. All that is known is that this faerie aided Meridell in the war against Darigan. Illusen lives in a glade in Meridell, and asks certain items from those who come to visit her. Those who bring her those items are said to receive great rewards.

Jhudora

One of the most mischievous faeries in existence, this dark faerie will inflict sickness, pestilence and bad luck on your Neopet if left unpleased. Residing in Faerieland, it is unknown why the Faerie Queen allows this dark faerie to conduct business in a city which is renowned for its good intentions and generous deeds. All that is known is that if you don't please this faerie, be prepared to pay the consequences, no matter how bad they are.

Space Faerie

In a galaxy far, far away, there exists a Space Faerie, the embodiment of all the cosmic power of good and just. The extent of her power is unknown, but she served tirelessly in the war against Dr. Sloth's evil bid for power in the early ages of Neopets' history and fought to free the enslavement of Grundos.

Battle Faerie

In times of great need, the Battle Faerie appears and aids those whose hearts are pure. Teaching the ancient forms of battle and strategy, any Neopet lucky enough to be graced by her presence will have their abilities

increased ten-fold. Whether or not this faerie truly exists is questionable, but ancient texts have made many references to periodic appearances made by this faerie and her steed named Legacy. Rumored to be a master of many disguises, appearances by this faerie have been very rare.

Jhuidah

Jhuidah, the cooking pot faerie resides on Mystery Island, where she guards her mixing pot. This magical pot has the ability to fuse two or more items together when mixed. If you can discover the secret combinations to mixing ingredients, powerful battledome weapons can be made.

Soup Faerie

A humanitarian faerie with the biggest heart, the soup faerie will provide free food to Neopets whose owners cannot afford to buy them any. With her soup kitchen located in Neopia Central, her cooking pots feed hundreds of thousands of Neopets every day.

Snow Faerie

The Snow Faerie lives on top of Terror Mountain, among the icy winds and frostbitten snow. Regarded as the

Jhuidah
Artwork by Katie Hartman

loses a tooth. What better way to use the tooth than to have it collected by the Tooth Faerie and receive some Neopoints in return! This is exactly what the tooth faerie does. If your pet's tooth is squeaky clean, expect great neopoint returns for the collection of that tooth.

Grey Faerie

The Grey Faerie is a faerie that lost her wings and was trapped by a dark faerie named Jennummara. Originally called Baelia, not much is known about this faerie except that she is on a quest to find another name to regain her wings and powers.

Normal Faeries

Normal faeries are abundant in Neopets. The most common forms are usually found bottled and sold in Kauvara's magic shop. Notorious for his faerie catching abilities, Balthazar, a bounty hunting Lupe is the main source of supply for these faeries. However, if your Neopet has that special factor and is quick enough, it will be able to sometimes catch faeries while you travel the lands of Neopia. Once in possession, these faeries will grant your Neopet a special ability in exchange for its freedom. Be forewarned – should your Neopet's level not be high enough, the faerie will be unable to bless it and will fly away.

Light Faerie

Bringer of hope in times of despair and sadness, this faerie's ability to turn wrong into right makes it a very popular faerie among many Neopets. Their sworn enemies are the dark faeries, who follow the light faeries' deeds uncannily, attempting to wrong every right the light faeries do. When these two elemental faeries confront each other, duck and take cover as the sparks fly!

Dark Faerie

Their mischievous ways hide their hidden agendas. Neopets shiver in fear each night before they go to bed, as their owners and parents tell them stories of how dark faeries lead weary

most popular holiday destination among neopians, due to its large visitor record, the Snow Faerie is one of the most accessible faeries in existence. If a person is kind enough to complete one of her requests, that person should expect to be rewarded handsomely.

Dung Faerie

Specific information about this faerie is unavailable. In addition, what this faerie looks like is unknown. The only proof of this faerie's existence is in the Meridell Rubbish Dump donations

credits list, which lists the Dung Faerie as a daily contributor.

Negg Faerie

Keeper of the much-coveted neggs, this faerie will buy and sell neggs, which have ranged effects from granting toys to increasing your Neopet's statistic points. While some of the neggs that she will trade can be a tad on the expensive side, she guarantees quality and endless supplies.

Tooth Faerie

Every now and again, your Neopet

travelers deeper into woods and forests where they become even more lost. It is widely known that these faeries should never, ever, be trusted. Sometimes desperate pets come to these faeries for aid – at a large price.

Earth Faerie

Concerned with anything to do with nature, these faeries are natural mothers and will ensure that nothing goes hungry. These faerie always strives for a delicate balance, believing

that a mixture of light and dark need to exist to keep everything in harmony and as they should be. Earth faeries will unite with the light faeries when they are losing a battle, then change sides and unite with the dark faeries

Snow Faerie
Artwork by Katie Hartman

when the dark faeries have the lower hand. More often than not however, these faeries keep to themselves, and refuse to take sides in the squabbles between the light and dark faeries.

Fire Faerie

Steamy, hot, fiery and passion to reach its goals are what the fire faeries are all about. Considered the coolest of the faeries, these powerful faeries are strong believers of getting out there to do what you want. Be careful if you approach these faeries, as if they are angered, they'll pay you back by setting fire to your clothes.

Air Faerie

Beauty and grace are what these faeries are all about. Nearly all of them possess long hair and graceful looks to match. Because they harness the power of the winds, they're extremely fast, and when confronted will vanish within a blink of an eye rather than meet the attacker head on.

Uber Faeries

Uber faeries are stronger versions of the normal faeries, and are the ones that will sometimes grant you quests when it requires certain items. If you complete the quests, they will reward one of your Neopets handsomely, by raising either its strength, defense, speed, intelligence or making it full. Refuse their quests however, and word will spread quickly throughout Faerieland and the faeries will hold you in disfavor, refusing to ask you for further quests for a period of time.

Light Faeries – Light Faeries ask you to find them trading cards, and will raise your pet's level.

Dark Faeries – Dark Faeries increase your pet's health points when you bring them toys.

Fire Faeries- Fire Faeries trade clothes for attack power.

Water Faeries – Water Faeries ask for books, and raise your pet's defense.

Air Faeries – Air Faeries want beauty products, and will bless your pet with speed.

Earth Faeries – Earth Faeries want magic items, and will feed your pet. ●

Site Spotlight
Further Reading
By Kym Huynh

One of the limitations of our first book is how much information can be placed inside it.

With such a large fan base, it is not surprising that there are thousands of Neopets fan sites on the Internet. One fan site you can visit for more information is PPT at http://www.pinkpt.com.

I recommend PPT for further reading to any reader here. Any strategy, solution or secret that exists on Neopets is listed here. This website is also extremely credible, and while not only providing lots of articles, hints, tips, solutions and secrets, it has very comprehensive sections on:

- How-not-to-get-scammed
- A reliable Battlepedia for all those veteran battlers
- A complete walk through for NeoQuest including full maps

PPT Air Faerie
Artwork by Katie Hartman

- A workshop with modeling instructions for all those art and craft junkies
- A large adoption agency
- And also one of the largest Neopets Community Forums

Other Noteworthy Fan Sites:
http://www.nothingbutNeopets.com/ Nothing But Neopets
http://www.Neopetsinfo.com/tno/ The Neopets Commentary
http://www.neoitems.net/ NeoItems
http://www.neononsense.net/ NeoNonsense

Neopets, Base Set Card Reviews

By: Scott Gerhardt

When I started reviewing these cards, more so than ever, I learned they have some of the same properties that so many card games before them have had - the game is very rare intensive. This means that the more rares you have, the better a deck you will often be able to make.

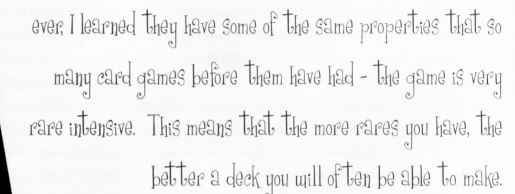

POJO'S CCG RATING SYSTEM

LAME

☆

COULD BE WORSE
☆☆

WORKS FOR ME

☆☆☆

SOLID ACTION

☆☆☆☆

FREAKIN' AWESOME!
☆☆☆☆☆

t's a very unfortunate circumstance of collectable card games (CCG) that the best cards are the ones that are hardest to get. However, the very nature of CCG – the best cards are in the most demand, and thus are harder to aquire. When reading the reviews, please remember that all cards were reviewed strictly on their playability and rarity was definitely not taken into account. While a card might need to be a 4 or 5 to be good if it's a rare, you may find that some commons and uncommons with ratings for 2.5 to 3 may be good for decks on a budget. We certainly understand that it can be difficult and expensive to always build the best deck, so be sure to look at some of the lower rating cards when you get into commons and uncommons, if you don't have a limitless supply of cards and money.

1
Aisha Myriad

"This card can be comboed, but is generally bad on its own. You don't need to cycle through your deck so fast with this. In general, find better Items"

★★★

2
Commander Garoo

"Not enough good stuff to be played. Solid stats, but rolls over to Earth. Air has better villains"

★★★½

3
The Darkest Faerie

"Now here is a villain that is vicious. Drawing a card isn't a horrible reward for defeat, 3 of it's 4 stats are good, and if you don't win, it hurts - a lot! This is definitely a great Dark Villain"

★★★★

4
The Ensorcellator

"This card is quite limited in use. Limiting it to two arenas, plus its ability only being slightly useful makes this card only playable in specialized decks."

★★★

5
Faerie Slingshot

Absolutely fantastic. This equipment helps anyone regardless of who it's on and makes any Neopet virtually unstoppable by anything less than a 6. Using it with returnable items makes it significantly broken.

★★★★½

6
Ferocious Negg

"Bad stats, but if you get lucky, it lets you search. Maybe this works well in some decks, but the bank would need to be at least 3 for me to consider this one."

★★½

7
Fire Shoyru

"Great for a Shoyru deck. Mostly good for getting rid of pesky Faerie Slingshots. Its stats aren't fantastic, but it can help even out a playing field. Play 1-2 with Shoyrus"

★★★★

8
Fyora the Faerie Queen

"She's almost always going to be a winner, but it costs you two Neopets to use her. There are usually better card advantage uses than her."

★★★

9
Ghost Lupe

"I'm not a big fan of this guy. He's dead in strength, only okay in Agility, making him only good half the time. His other stats aren't great, and the bonus, not that superb to being with, only works on your turn. I'll pass"

★★½

10
Grarrl Gladiator

"In my opinion, one of the best experienced pets there is. Sure, he only has one good stat, but that stat is almost always a winner. Even if he gets thrown somewhere bad, he will win a third of the time. In a game of die rolls, doubling your chances is amazing."

★★★★★

11
Grimoire of Thade

"Great, solid stats, and the bank ability is fantastic. If you're playing 4 or more experienced Neopets, you can't beat getting a bank point and drawing 2 cards. Wonderful!"

★★★★½

12
Hubrid Nox

"Two good stats, two bad ones. Water rolls over Hubrid, and it's only really that fantastic in intelligence. If Fire really needs a villain, I guess this one will work."

★★★

13
Hubrid Nox Statue

"Don't trick yourself - this thing is only a bank value of three, and only if you have a Puzzle Box there. It requires Dark to play, and the stat bonuses are okay. You won't generally be able to make this card work well."

★★½

14
Illusen

"She is a good solid reset, allowing you to put all your Earth Neopets where they need to be. Good for earth heavy decks, but somewhat limited outside of that."

★★★★½

15
Illusen's Staff

"If you can focus on Magic and Intelligence, this is a solid card. It gives a decent Magic bonus and a variable, but large intelligence bonus that makes it useful in the right deck."

★★★★½

16
Jeran

"This has an interesting lure effect. If you play it right against the right deck, you can completely clear other arenas so your Neopets get a clear shot. Jeran might play the sacrificial lamb, but it's good to play into an arena with a villain, nailing down an opponent's turn. Against Dark, he's fantastic. Not great otherwise."

★★★½

17
Jhudora

"She slows the game down immensely. Two fantastic stats make her a hard-to-penetrate ""wall"". All players will have a hard time banking with her down. The win condition is pretty good, though. You might be able to set up a good condition of having her stall, then self-defeating her. Look for combos here."

★★★★½

18
Jhudora's Wand

"I'm quite scared by this card. If you can play it with other cards that refill you hard quickly, it's not a bad fast play. It will utterly own the Magic and Intelligence arenas, but at a tremendous cost. If you can play it the early-to-mid game, it could be a winner, but you don't want to play it late."

★★★½

19
Kadoatie

"This will help keep your light deck well rounded. It gives solid, but not broken bonuses to any arena. It's playable if you're trying to stay well-rounded in a utility deck."

★★★★

20
Korbat Researcher

"Lower stats, but if you keep him in the right place, it allows you to really sift though your deck fast. Use him with books that already have drawing effects upon banking, and you'll build a quality hand in no time. Don't go overboard, but 2 of these with Korbats is good."

★★★★

21
Lord Darigan

"Not a bad stat in the house, and it makes all your Dark Neopets a little big stronger. This may be my favorite villain because it's a wall you just can't seem to get through, while giving you a chance to break through other places with the stat bonuses."

22
Magnus the Torch

"It's fire's only good hero, but that doesn't mean Fire should play with heroes"

23
Malevolent Sentient Poogle Plushie

"Good 'ole MSPP is the ultimate in slaughtering Villains. If you're against a lot of Villains, this is your man. Even against other Neopets, it's pretty solid, usually giving you an opening stat advantage. If playing Dark or Water, I recommend 2-3 in every deck."

24
Master Vex

"A decent Hero, but provides very little towards a major advantage. Not great against Villains, and can still be outstatted or outitemed against other Neopets. There are definitely better heroes"

25
Moltenore

The Petpet for fire with the same similar effect Kadoatie has for light. It will keep you rounded and give your Neopets a shot in any arena.

26
Rainbow Paint Brush

"If this card allowed the experienced to go into hand, I would be jumping for joy over it. As it is, it gains no card advantage, only library manipulation. There are plenty of ways to draw cards, and the stat bonuses don't make it worth playing"

27
Rainbow Swirly Thing

"This is pretty bad. If gives few bonuses on its own and requires you to win with a 6 to even have a good effect. Searching is good, but it's not worth it to only search 1 in 6 times. At least it has an okay bank value."

28
Siyana of Taldor

"She's great against Dark, and will probably take out most Villains and a lot of Dark Neopets. She's a solid hero for light."

29
Vira

"With decent stats, it's really nothing special, but the Villain of choice for both air and water players."

30
Vira's Dagger

"You're not going to catch me dead playing this. The bank is only 2, the effect if marginal, and it's uses limited, and it's swap around ability not as good as advertised. There is better, and I'll play with it."

31
Blue Poogle

"Poogles are generally the strongest basic type, and this is the best Poogle. Solid stats in all 4 arenas, plus much beefier on your turn."

 ☆☆☆☆☆

32
Blue Shoyru

"One excellent and 3 decent arenas. Against Earth it's great. Otherwise, simply solid"

 ☆☆☆☆

33
Green Kacheek

Two strong arenas and good against prevalent dark rivals. A good basic.

 ☆☆☆½

34
Red Grarrl

"Not that great, but needed for Grarrl decks, and the best Grarrl basic."

 ☆☆☆

35
Red Lupe

Good against Air and has 3 solid arenas. Nice in general.

 ☆☆☆½

36
Yellow Poogle

"Only slightly less good than Blue Poogle, it has more rounded stats, and better against fire. Still great."

 ☆☆☆☆½

37
Acara Acrobat

"This card is overly agility focused, and even that stat isn't that great. This card should be in the Agility arena, making it's ability close to useless."

 ☆☆

38
Acara Treasure Seeker

"This is a far better Experienced for Acara. It's stats are generally better, and it's ability is better. Being able to reroll that chance for a 6, or being able to cancel out that 1 can be quite useful."

 ☆☆☆☆

39
Aisha Enchantress

"A couple of decent stats, and it's ability is really good, especially with boomerang items. It's a decent Experienced for Aisha, but certainly not overly strong."

 ☆☆☆½

40
Apple Lantern

"If you're playing fruit heavy, it's quite nice, as it can often give you 1-2 cards in hand, plus a bank of two. Combine that with a solid strength bonus and it's quite playable."

 ☆☆☆☆

41
Balthazar

"Quite a nice Villain. Faerie's can't touch it, and it has decent stats. Good for earth"

42
Battle Eyrie

"This card is ridiculous. The stats aren't that great, but it more than makes up for it with the fact you can roll two dice. It doubles your chances of an auto-win and can make your stats pretty solid. This card is an auto for Eyries and a really solid experienced."

43
Brain Tree Root

"Great intelligence bonus and can move a rival. If it did one more thing, I'd recommend it. As it is, it's only good, not great."

44
Cackling Negg

"There are good Negg decks out there, and this goes in it. It can simply win a contest for you late. Not good unless you're playing the Negg deck, but you need probably 2-3 copies of this in the Negg deck."

45
"Calabrus, Cloud Aisha"

"It's alright if you don't have access to holos. Otherwise, not that good."

46
Cardboard Enemy

"This only has some possible good effects if you're playing Villains with negative loss conditions, like The Darkest Faerie. In general, though, it's quite a bad card."

47
Copier v2.0

"A good defensive card, but generally only good when your back is against the wall. You should build your deck to win, not to prevent losing."

48
Darigan's Blight

"A nice card if your deck is Villain dependent. Sometimes, this will do nothing for your opponent. If you rely on Villains and are going fire, it's very good."

49
Dark Faerie Sisters

"Really bad stats for a Villain. I know they're popular, but they're really bad."

50
Dissent

This is a downright horrible circumstantial card. Please don't play it.

51
Eliv Thade

"It's basically good in Intelligence, and maybe Magic, but the defeat effect is bad. I probably would not chance it with him."

★★½

52
Ghost Korbat

This a weird wall. Keep it out of Strength and it will make for a good deterrent to your opponent. It's worth playing in Korbat decks.

★★★★

53
The Giant Grarrl

Way too focused to be good for a hero. A hero should have at least 3 stats in double digits - this has 1.

★½

54
Grarrl Guard

"If it weren't for Grarrl Gladiator, this card would be really good. Unfortunately, the Gladiator is simply superior."

★★★★

55
How to Cheat

"In a book-heavy deck, this is ridiculous. Adding library manipulation would be helpful to make sure you don't get stuck."

★★★★

56
Hubrid's Puzzle Box

"An obvious piece for the statue, but okay on it's own. In the late game, it's pretty good for bonuses, but I think you'll generally find better cards."

★★★

57
Illusen's Ring

"Definitely a metagame card. If people around you are playing a lot of Air or Dark, it's good. Otherwise, probably not worth the slot."

★★★

58
Jerdana

"A potential Villain slaughterer, just like her Orb. A very good answer to Villains."

★★★★

59
Jerdana's Orb

"Solid banking and some solid stats. On top of that, it massacres villains. If you're Dark and Water, you'd play MSPP in this slot. Otherwise, this is a fantastic villain slaughtering device."

★★★★

60
Jhudora's Storm

"It's okay because of the order they happen in. This can cause a lot of shifting to happen that is very positive to you. In a tricky deck, I can see it seeing some use."

★★★½

61
Kacheek Thief

"The stats for this guy are okay at best, and it's not that often you're going to win without a rival, especially if this is in play. When it does work, though, it's quite good."

62
Kauvara's Potion

"If you have Earth, it can't be bad. It gives great Magic stats on it's own, but it can become something else if need be. Playing this will almost never be bad - look for a lot of combos with it."

63
"Koya, Korbat Huntress"

"She is very good at establishing order of cards for things that work with it, and is an okay Hero. Use it for it's manipulation ability and then abuse it with other cards."

64
Lucky Coin

"Gives library manipulation, but not card advantage. It's stats aren't good enough to play, and it's only real good point is a bank of three. We can do much better."

65
MAGAX: Destroyer

"Not good in the mirror match, and it's stats aren't all that great. Probably better villains to play."

66
Magic Lottery Ticket

"It works one time out of six. Please, please play something better."

67
Meuka

This card is trash. Don't play it.

68
Mirror Shield

"Quite nice, as it will nullify your opponent playing items, as well as give a solid intelligence bonus. This is good if you're playing with Neopets already having great stats."

69
Morphing Runes

Ugh. Why are your Neopets in the wrong arena to begin with? This is a horrible loss of card advantage and seldom good.

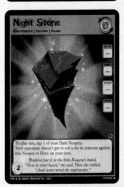

70
Night Stone

"This card gives you a variable 1 to 6 bonus every turn, plus eliminates the possibility of an auto-win for your opponent on your turn. It's kind of limited since it only works on your turn and gives no bonuses, but it would work very well with the ""boomerang"" items."

71
Noil

"Three great stats, but a 6 and you lose him. Things that can go away quickly don't make me too happy. Probably not your best bet, but he is very cute."

72
Poogle Racer

"I love this guy. Strength and Agility are both decent players here, and the ability to shift makes it good to run into an empty arena and steal a win, or be able to "block" a rival and still try to take one from him before his turn. Quite an amazing experienced."

73
Potion of Sludge

"It only works one in six times, but it gives a solid Magic bonus on it's own. Definitely playable in fire, but it's not that good."

74
Pressure-Pad Puzzle

"First of all, why would you put 3 Neopets in one arena? This sets your opponent up for far greater card advantage by clearing out arenas. I'd say it's decent with Poogle Racers, and maybe it's okay in a light/water deck, but that is it unless you use something like Jhudora's Storm afterwards."

75
Red Clockwork Grundo

"A nice little insurance policy. If you don't win, but you're close, you can ditch the Grundo and give yourself the win. Could be nice in situations where the game is close."

76
Red Scorchstone

"Like Illusen's Ring. If the metagame calls for this, play it. Otherwise, not worth it."

77
Scorchio Warrior

"This isn't too bad because it allows you bring it down with some beef. It requires you to be more equipment heavy, but the increased speed of not having to tap it down for a turn is very nice. A solid experienced with a couple of solid stats."

78
Scroll of Recall

"This is a great card. A good bank with it yielding card advantage in the form of returning cards. I can't think of an earth deck that would not play this, and play 3 of them."

79
Shadow Usul

"Um, why? Seriously, the stats aren't great, and you have to keep discarding to play out a bad villain. No."

80
Slorg Trails

"A solid ""Stasis""-like effect. If you can keep your pets clear of filled arenas, this could lead to some serious card advantage. This is another card that works ridiculously well with Jhudora's Storm."

81
Sloth's Master Plan

"It's Earth's answer to villains. I think there are generally better answers, but it does wipe the board completely, so it's good if there are 2+ Villains on the board."

★★★

86
Thyora's Tear

See Illusen's Ring and Red Scorchstone

★★★

82
Spyder

I don't really like effects that only happen on a 6 unless the card is good on it's own. This does little to give bonuses and only works one-sixth of the time. There are much better cards for the slot.

★★½

87
Tinka

It's a problem not being able to go against Dark when you're a hero. This seems too circumstantial to be good.

★★

83
Spyder Bites

An item that rewards losing? No thank you.

★½

88
Tishi and Goliath

"This card can really hose over villains but putting them places they don't need to be. If villains are in your metagame, this is a really good card to have."

★★★★

84
Striped Negg

"Great on it's own outside of a Negg deck. Even in a Negg deck, it's still a bank of 4. Highly playable."

★★★★½

89
"Torshac, Shoyru Scout"

"This hero is absolutely amazing with boomerang items. You're completely protected against a 6, and can play them only as needed. Decent stats too. Too bad it's a hero."

★★★★

85
Sword of the Air Faerie

"Slightly better than Illusen's Ring and Red Scorchstone since it can be moved and gives +3, but still quite limited since it's only good against Earth. It's a possibility, though."

★★★½

90
Traveling Library

"This takes card advantage to a whole new level. The light/book deck makes this thing really sick. Combo with Cleansing Flames for a ridiculous, game ending effect."

★★★★★

91
Wand of Nova

"This is what we call a counterspell. It will stop things from happening at a 1 to 1 ratio, which isn't bad. It banks well and also has good Agility and Magic stats. This is a very solid card."

92
Werelupe King

"Good grief, Balthazar is a billion times better than this. Don't play this unless you can't find a Balthazar"

93
Wocky Beast

"Tremendous Anti-Light, but that's the only time it's good. Maybe used in the strength arena make it strong enough to play on it's own, but somewhat conditional, but strong under those conditions."

94
Woodland Bow

Ugh! Only adds to one stat and not enough to make it worth playing.

95
Yellow Clockwork Grundo

"Just like the Red Clockwork Gundo, only yellow!"

96
Zombify

"It trades card advantage, and is generally not good, but could have it's uses in a very aggressive-style deck."

97
Air Faerie Token

The bankability and the chance of this making you unstoppable in agility makes it a sufficient double-threat.

98
Aisha Slogrider

This thing is horrible. I can't say much more.

99
"Big, Heavy Sword"

"If they already have good strength, do they need a lot more? No."

100
Biting Book

"One of the best uncommons in the set. Being able to cycle through your deck for quality is really nice, especially with a bank of 2."

101
Blue Paint Brush

"The Intelligence brush. They are all good for utility to keep the right ratio of Neopets out there. Not required, but good for tempo and at least have a bank of more than 1."

102
Bottle of Grarrl

"It banks for 4, that's about all I can say positive about it."

103
Cleansing Flames

"Niceness. This allows you to play more efficient 1 bank value cards, then all at once, switch out everything with stuff that is better bank value. Good combo potential."

104
Dark Faerie Token

"Probably the best Charm - gives a little to all stats, gives a little more for Dark, and banks for 4. Very nice."

105
Dogglefox

Stats are not good enough to justify the effect.

106
Earth Faerie Leaves

The perfect addition to the boomerang item deck. Play this with Faerie Slingshot and boomerang items and you have a sick combo that works without fear.

107
Earth Faerie Token

"The same as Air Faerie Token - decent, not great."

108
Everlasting Apple

It's a boomerang card. They are almost all good. Playable to make up Intelligence and Strength gaps.

109
"Everything, Volume 1"

"It's a book that helps intelligence or banks on it. Situational, but in the right deck is really solid."

110
Evil Sloth Clone #238

This is great! You can search out more copies of a bad villain and get them out of your deck as fast as possible. There really are better cards out there.

111
Eyrie Guard

An annoying wall as it can be very hard to get through in a defensive deck. Play it in your Eyrie deck.

112
Faerie Lantern

Very non-interesting. It should have banked for more.

113
Faerie Pancakes

"Very interesting, as you have to win 1 before it takes effect. On the whole, though, it has good Strength and Agility bonuses and banks well with a bonus once it does. A good utility card."

114
Farlax V

"Well, if you're going light, this is your only Villain option, and it's bad. If you must have a villain, I guess, but I don't think light should be playing with Villains."

115
Fire Faerie Token

No better or worse than the Air and Earth Tokens.

116
Fumble!

This a bad card in general. It's too reliant on other things to be good.

117
General Kass

These uncommon Heroes are just not as good as their rare counter-parts

118
The Golden Shoyru

"I guess it's decent to manipulate your library when you can bank for 3. Much better with Shoyru since it allows combos with stuff like How to Cheat then, but okay on it's own."

119
Grey Faerie

"Almost playable in the right situation, this makes everything vanilla for a turn. If you need to play some off-color stuff, this would allow it, but only for one turn. "

120
Hidden Tower Secrets

"This card was a mistake at an uncommon. This should easily be rare, and is absolutely ridiculous. If you play books, you must play this."

121
Jeran's Sword

"Combine it with the Armor for a pretty solid combo. Not great on it's own, but solid comboed"

126
Mavara's Wocky

UGH! The only purpose is to add dark to a fire Wocky deck. Next please.

⭐½

122
Juppies

It takes more than a bank of 4 to be good.

127
Mirgle

"Actually decent for an uncommon, but only goes on experienced. That makes it more limited."

123
Kacheek Shepherd

"This is the only saving grace to making Petpets playable, and it still has to go a ways to do it."

128
Mynci Inventor

"While the stats aren't great, the ability to draw from banking equipment make this worth looking at. You're going to have to boost his stats, though."

124
Light Faerie Token

"Just like the Dark version, just usually less targets for it. Still does the good distribution and high bank"

129
Mynci Tourist

So you've got a lot of Agility. That don't impress me much.

⭐½

125
Lupe Defender

"An experienced need to be a little better than this. It's okay, but not great"

⭐⭐½

130
Nothing Has Happened

"It's a counterspell (Magic reference). It will stop any Something Has Happened, so it's good to pack them if you have water and people are playing SHH cards, something most people are."

131
Nova

"Has a nice sac ability to counter out an item, but probably not worth playing."

⭐⭐½

132
Pawkeet

"Gets cute points, but another situational Petpet. Most Petpets aren't that worth playing, so the ones conditional on others will likewise not be that good."

⭐⭐½

133
Poogle Apprentice

Anything that requires you to have multiple Neopets in the contest to be good is simply not good.

⭐⭐

134
Put On Display

"This is a very interesting card. You can win with your own equipment by dropping it into the bank, or force an equipment off an opponent by giving them some bank points. This is a better card than more people will give it credit for."

⭐⭐⭐⭐½

135
Red Paint Brush

The strength brush. Just like the Blue one.

⭐⭐⭐⭐½

136
Ring of the Summoner

"So this thing brings in Villains to the arena it's in? Yeah, it can hurt your opponent too, but that's really not that smart in my opinion."

⭐½

137
Scabu

"Okay, most of this fruit is bad on it's own. You have to go theme with it to be good."

⭐⭐

138
Scorchio Alchemist

This allows you to basically play an extra item if you feel necessary. It's really a decent Scorchio.

⭐⭐⭐⭐½

139
Shoyru Spy

"Looking at your opponent's hand is good an all, but I don't think that's enough to justify the lower overall stats."

⭐⭐½

140
Silver Negg

"If you know your opponent it kind of item low, then this should be a winner for you. Even without the bonus, it's solid with good stats and worth a couple in the bank."

⭐⭐⭐⭐

141
Sludging Ray

"This is disgustingly bad. Three for one card disadvantage only works in Pokemon, not in Neopets"

146
Spooky Beans

"At best, okay. Moving people around is nice, but really not that great in general unless you're building an entire deck abound it."

142
Slumberberry Potion

This can yield good advantage on your opponent's turn if you win by stopping 2 attacks with 1 Item. Add in the bank value and we have a player.

147
Take a Dip

"If this put the card in hand, it would be great. Instead, it goes on top of your library. I guess if you were desperate, it would work, but I'm not a fan of it."

143
Snorkle

"An okay Petpet that basically will allow you to play another item during the turn if it's food by giving +3 to all stats. One of the better Petpets, but that still doesn't mean it makes the main deck. Maybe in food-based decks."

148
Thingy

"This yields bankable advantage, which is good - even if it does get a Petpet. If you can find an instance to play it, it's good."

144
Snowball Cannon

I still loathe things that require you to roll a six to be good. This is another one of those.

149
Traveling Neopia

"It's a book with sick stats in intelligence. Truth known, there are better books."

145
Speckled Negg

"In the Negg deck, this is sick. Four to all stats, and the bank can be 3. Wowsers that's nice."

150
Turmaculus Strikes!

This thing whacks a Petpet. This is way too circumstantial for me.

151
Water Faerie Token

See the other 3 elemental tokens.

★★★

152
Weakness

A single turn reduction.
Eewwwww.

★

153
Werelupe Sage

"Stats are okay at best. This is one of those ""budget"" Villains"

★★½

154
Wocky Farmer

"The only way vegetables can be good, Funny enough, most vegetables have such a high bank value, that this thing will never get too big."

★★

155
Yellow Negg

"This will allow you to win fast in the Negg deck. You can get the job done in 6 banks if done right. This is quite playable, especially with the nice little stats."

★★★★

156
Yellow Paint Brush

"The Agility brush. Still gives tempo, still slightly playable."

★★★★½

157
Blue Aisha

"All in all, probably the weakest Aisha. It's stats are tied for a combined best, but is very non-complimentary to the other two."

★★★

158
Blue Kacheek

"The stats are comparable to it's green counterpart, but lacks the special ability, making it clearly weaker."

★★★

159
Blue Lupe

"A little less rounded than the Red version, it's still okay with three solid arenas. This makes Lupe one of the more playable basics."

★★★

160
Blue Wocky

"This one is close, but I tend to go with a more rounded Neopet rather than a disbalanced one since you do have to play 3 arenas, not just one. By a whisker, this rather solid Neopet makes my list as the top Wocky."

★★★½

161
Green Eyrie

"I've got this as the best Eyrie, but it's close. I hate only having 1 stat over 4, but it's good having 3 over 2, which I feel is very important when you're going to play with 3 arenas usually."

★★★½

162
Green Grarrl

"Grarrls are simply a bad basic type. Though their experienced are very nice. This one it like the Green, only with the token +1 to Magic, but lacks the Light bonus. Only play 1 of these after you have 3 Red in your deck."

★★½

163
Green Korbat

"The ""complimentary"" Korbat, it goes best with the superior Yellow Korbat. It's close, has the beefy strength, and is solid in 3 arenas. It also has the best combined stats. Overall, not a bad choice."

★★★

164
Green Mynci

"Overall stronger than the Yellow Mynci, but does not work as well in conjunction with the Blue Mynci, which means I would put this one on the bench and keep him there."

★★½

165
Green Wocky

"Close to Blue Wocky, and might make the cut over the Blue one if your deck is strength weak and better in the Magic department. This is a call based on what your deck is like."

★★★

166
Red Acara

This one is a toss-up with it's yellow counterpart. This one probably best complements the superior green one with the higher Magic and a slightly higher strength. I would play this second based on that.

★★★

167
Red Eyrie

"This is a close second to Green Eyrie, as it has the strongest top stats in strength and agility, but really gives up the other 2 arenas."

★★★

168
Red Scorchio

"While this is a solid basic, it's just the worst of the Scorchios. The addition to Intelligence does not counter for the sub-par agility. It's close, but you should not give up arenas you don't have to."

★★★

169
Red Shoyru

"This Neopet does not have an overly weak arena, with a minimum 4 in each. I still would play Blue over Red just because I don't feel the +1 to Magic overrides the +2 against earth, but it's pretty close to a toss up."

★★★★

170
Yellow Acara

"About as good as Red Acara, but does not seem to fit the Acara deck well."

★★½

171
Yellow Aisha

"The worst Aisha on it's own, but the stats best compliment the Red Aisha, making it my secondary Aisha in an Aisha deck."

★★½

172
Yellow Korbat

"This wins the Korbat race with two very strong 6 arenas. It also has that bare bones score of 3 in Agility, which makes is playable in that arena."

★★★½

173
Yellow Mynci

"Technically, I would call this the worst Mynci, but it works best with the Blue Mynci, so it would be played with it in a complementary role. This should definitely not be in your first three, though."

★★

174
Yellow Scorchio

"Our King Scorchio. With all stats high enough, and two above 6, this one is generally the greatest overall threat."

★★★★

175
Asparagus

"It's a standard common Veggie - high bank, low stats."

★★

176
Babaa

We're into the dregs of Petpets

★½

177
Beyond Neopia

Great pluses and banking gives you a card. This is a very good card to play.

★★★½

178
Blue Negg

"Decent stats, plus the chance of increasing its worth, is a good thing."

★★★

179
Book of Sadness

"While it's not that bad, there are better books. Look to this one for a bank value."

★★½

180
Broken Sword

"Good to off Slingshots, but not much else."

★★½

181
Brown Negg

"Not one of your better Neggs, but probably needed in the Negg deck."

 ★★½

182
Bubble Gun

This is not a good card - at all

★

183
Buzzer Swarm

"Okay, they can't bank a card - they'll just draw one. Disgusting."

★

184
Capture the Snowbunnies

"If you're going to play Petpets, play this. I just don't recommend playing Petpets right now."

★★½

185
Charming the Miamice

"If your opponent is playing Petpets, this is just sickeningly good. I just don't think it's a good idea to plan for your opponent to be playing Petpets"

★★

186
Chocolate Korbats

"It's a standard misdirection card - keep moving those Neopets around, but to what end?"

★★½

187
Chokato

Back to the Veggies - this one at least gives +2 to Strength

★★

188
Chomp!

"If you need a finisher, Chomp! will get the job done. Instead of using an item to up your stats, you can use this card to kill your opponent's stats. Actually playable, and would be more so if you could bank it."

★★★

189
Defence Shield v1.0

A terrible piece of equipment

★

190
Elixir of Thieves

Nothing special agility booster. At least a lot of these commons banks for good value.

★★

191
Escape Rope

"More misdirection. This could be useful to some end since you can move it while playing it, which seems to be the better play most of the time."

 ★★★

192
Essence of Brain

"Boomerang Item, which makes it good. This one has good intelligence, which is nice and the solid bank value. Very playable."

 ★★★★

193
Eyrie Breastplate

"This card is downright bad when attached to a non-Eyrie, and is only marginal on an Eyrie. I don't think this should see much play."

 ★★

194
Faerie Dishwater

"A magical boomerang card. Every boomerang card is playable, especially if they have things to compliment them."

 ★★★★

195
Gigantic Snowball

"This card really isn't the best in card advantage, and I don't recommend it."

★½

196
Golden A

"This card might be playable if you have Aishas. Even at that, probably not. Good if you need bank numbers."

 ★★½

197
Green Negg

"Almost as good as the Blue Negg, but once again, good in the Negg deck."

 ★★★

198
Happy Negg

"This card is amazing in the Negg deck, as it allows you to play out your Neggs without as much fear of not being able to bank them later. I would always play 3 of these in a Negg deck, but obviously little use outside the Negg deck."

 ★★★★

199
Harris

"One of the better common Petpets, but still bad."

★★½

200
Hasee

Just as bad as Babaa

★½

201
Ice Scimitar

"Can pile on the strength if needed, but not generally playable"

★★

206
Jhudora's Evil Eye

"It's at least one for one card advantage, so that's not too bad, and it's generally going to be in your advantage quality-wise. I just can't justify recommending a discard card in a game where card advantage can be so prevalent."

★★½

202
Icy Snowball

There really are better cards than this.

★½

207
Korbat's Cape

"I guess it's okay with Korbats, but it's still only +4 Magic there. Maybe for the 3 bank it's okay - just not fantastic."

★★½

203
Illusen's Charm

"It's hard to recommend this card when the Dark and Light charms are so much better, even outside Dark and Light decks."

★

208
Lab Ray

I simply can not figure out a good reason to play this card at all.

★

204
Jelly Aishas

"At least this card replaces itself. Unfortunately, it needs some stronger stats, and it doesn't replace itself when played. It's decent, but certainly not that good."

★★½

209
Library Visit

A must for all light decks. Every last deck that is prominently light must play 3 copies of this.

★★★★★

205
Jeran's Armor

"This is a beacon of light in the dregs of the commons. It's not great for stats, but shutting down items can certainly be a major plus for you. With the Sword, this is a somewhat formidable combo."

★★★

210
Lisha's Glasses

Not all that great. Needs to have some other kind of ability

★½

211
Meowclops

"Another good budget Petpet, but not for non-cheap decks."

 ★★½

212
Misdirection

"This is a better card than meets the eye. You can use it to set up two favorable match-ups, and then your opponent will have to spend a turn getting those match-ups fixed, usually resulting in at least ""even"" to as much as ""4 times"" card advantage."

★★★★

213
Money Tree Ghosts

"Very situational to play, and the effect is at best, marginal."

★

214
Moon Charm

Once again we go back to Dark and Light charms being better

★

215
Pant Devil Attacks

"While I do not recommend the random discard effect, this one might be a little better, as stripping away an item, especially boomerang items, can be brutally good."

★★★

216
Peachpa

"Good effects, but scary because it's pointless if your opponent plays an item. You might be able to play this card well, playing it around your opponents' items, but I don't think it would usually make the cut."

★★

217
Petpetnip

"If you're brave enough to play with the Petpets, this card could easily make the deck, especially because of it's high bank value. "

★★★

218
Pinanna

It's one of those lower-end fruit-type cards.

★½

219
Potatoes

It's one of those lower-end veggie-type cards.

★

220
Potion of Speed

"Another great Boomerang item. This one adds to agility, which is nice."

★★★½

221
Potion of Strength

"Just as good as the speed potion, and just as playable."

★★★½

222
Purrow's Plight

"It's an item that affects all intelligence for one turn. Unfortunately, this usually means it will only help 1 Neopet. We'll pass on this one."

★½

223
Sceptre of Banishing

"A common answer to Villains, it's actually decent. "

★★★

224
Secret Passage

"This is a good card to set up some favorable match-ups, get around Villains quickly, maybe score some fast cards or banking, or simply get out of a mess your opponent has put you in. A nice little weapon."

★★★★

225
Shadow Breeze

I would not really suggest this as a potion of choice.

★½

226
Snowbunny

"Another one of those bad Petpets, though bunnies are cute."

★½

227
Starberry

There sure are a lot of lower-end fruit cards.

★½

228
Stone Snowball

"The snowballs aren't very good, not even in a theme deck."

★½

229
The Thieves' Code

Banking and drawing is definitely nice. The stats certainly make it worth it as well.

★★★½

230
Turnips

This is another disgustingly bad veggie.

★

231
Usica Berries

And the parade of bad fruit continues.

232
Wand of Confusion

"I'm kind of confused why I would play this. Maybe in an all-common deck, but that's it."

233
Warf

"Bad Petpet, need I say more?"

234
Wooden Blocking Shield

"Bad equipment overall, and I won't say any more."

S1
Blue Mynci

"Usually a 1 or 2 in an arena means you're giving up on it. All Myncis are 2 or less in both strength and magic. Checking the other 2 more pertinent stats, this makes this Mynci the best of one of the worst basic types."

★★★

S2
Red Korbat

"It's a Holo, and it's the weakest. It gives up on two arenas with 2 arenas being good. Overall, it's just not the best Korbat."

★★½

S3
Blue Scorchio

"This basic concedes no arenas, but is weaker on overall stats than the strongest Yellow version, but is superior to the Red, which does lack in Agility."

★★★½

S4
Green Acara

"The best Acara, it has better combined stats than the other two, and is the most rounded, with only 1 weak area. I would generally start an Acara deck with 3 of these."

★★★½

S5
Red Aisha

"This has the best combined stats, but gives up the Agility completely for at least respectable Strength, which makes it a major threat in 2 arenas and a minor in 1."

★★★½

S6
Yellow Eyrie

"A bit worse the Red version, it still gives up 2 arenas and has a weaker strength. The differences are subtle, but they can cost you a game."

★★½

Dark Deck Construction 101

By: Paul Hagan

Have you ever had a problem getting the right type of Faerie symbol on the board? Have you ever been stuck with a lot of Fire cards in your hand, but the only Neopets you have in your arenas are Water? Don't you hate when that happens? One of the best ways to avoid such a situation is to pilot a deck with just one Faerie type. The focus of this article is on doing just that.

We'll start off by choosing one of the six Faerie types. Just browsing through cards, it looks like Dark offers a lot of options in the way of stripping your opponent's hand, playing solid Villains, manipulating your opponent's Neopets and most importantly, having a great set of Neopets.

Neopet Stack

Now that we have chosen Dark as our Faerie type, there are five options available for our Neopet stack: Red Grarrl, Red Korbat, Green Grarrl, Green Korbat, and Yellow Korbat.

We'll leave out the Yellow Korbat since its highest stat in any arena is just a 6. That way, whenever you draw a Korbat, you are guaranteed an 8 in Intelligence and at least a 4 in Magic. Both Grarrls will provide you with a 9 in Strength no matter what,

with the Red Grarrls getting a +2 in all stats against Light rivals.

Items

Hubrid's Puzzle Box doesn't grant any bonuses on its own, but gives +1 to each Stat for each card in your opponent's bank. It also interacts well with Hubrid Nox Statue, which not only gives +5 to all stats, but it can also pull cards out of your opponent's bank.

Dark Faerie Token doesn't really have any special reasoning behind it being included in the deck. It gives +2 across each stat in this deck and it banks for 4 Neopoints. You can't ask for a much better all-around utility card.

A single copy of Jhudora's Wand has been included in the deck. The card can be massively fun and will swing a contest in your favor, but rarely is it worth giving up your entire hand for it.

The last item, Potion of Strength, is

not a Dark card, but the potential to win every contest unless your opponent rolls a 6 is too good to pass up.

Equipment

Night Stone, although it does not give any stat bonuses, prevents your opponent from rolling any dice in a contest on your turn. This can completely wreck your opponent's game plan, and it stops them from winning by rolling a 6.

One of this deck's two weak areas is in the Magic arena. With six Korbats in your Neopet stack, Korbat Cape's increase to Magic by +4 is worth adding in.

As one of the deck's major focuses is manipulating your opponent's creatures, Spyder's ability to keep your opponent's Neopets tapped down is valuable.

Something Has Happened!

Dark is very good at hand manipulation. Jhudora's Evil Eye and Pant

Devil attacks both help strip your opponent's hand of any useful cards that he or she may be hiding, and it forces your opponent to draw a card whenever they win a contest, as opposed to banking to get ahead.

Chomp! should also be included on the deck list, as it allows your Neopets to break through a tough-to-win contest. Keep in mind that you don't have many enhancement cards to Strength and Intelligence, so Chomp! can be a nice surprise after an opponent stacks one of his Neopets with a lot of Equipment to even the match up.

Villains

With the high Strength and Intelligence, the only contests that the Dark player should worry about are Agility and Magic.

Shadow Usul allows you to completely dominate an arena. With a 19 Agility and the ability to return to its owners hand instead of being discarded when it is defeated, the Shadow Usul belongs in almost every Dark deck.

The only other villain worth major consideration in this deck is The Darkest Faerie. Although she does not return to her owner's hand when defeated, she does send defeated

Basic Neopets to the bottom of their owner's Neopet stack, or she can discard Experienced Neopets and Heroes.

Heroes

This deck almost doesn't have room for any Heroes, but two were included just because they can always serve as a quick surprise near the end of the game to swing the tide in your favor.

The Giant Grarrl provides you with an instant-speed, high Strength combatant that will almost always win in the Strength arena. Koya, Korbat Huntress doesn't have any incredibly high stats, but she comes with the ability to stack the top of your deck, making playing at least one copy of her more than worthwhile.

Experienced Neopets

Because of our item and equipment choices, two of the Experienced Neopets are not of any use. Korbat Researcher is not of much use without any Books, and with no Weapons or Armors, Grarrl Guard is not very useful either.

However, Ghost Korbat's ability to manipulate your opponent's Neopets claims it a spot in your deck instantly. Grarrl Gladiator wins his spot because of its ability to win 1 in 3 of all of your contests, no matter what.

Playing the Deck

This deck is incredibly simple to play. Make sure that you control the Strength arena with Grarrls and the Intelligence arena with Korbats. Use additional Korbats equipped with Korbat Cape to hold off your opponent's Neopets in the Magic arena, or if none are available, play a Villain in that arena. Accept that you won't win in the Agility arena and just keep a Shadow Usul there at all times.

Neopet Stack

3 **Red Grarrl**
1 **Green Grarrl**
3 **Red Korbat**
3 **Green Korbat**

Deck

3 **Night Stone**
3 **Korbat Cape**
3 **Spyder**
1 **Jhudora's Wand**
3 **Dark Faerie Token**
3 **Hubrid's Puzzle Box**
3 **Hubrid Nox Statue**
2 **Potion of Strength**
3 **Jhodora's Evil Eye**
3 **Pant Devil Attacks**
2 **Chomp!**
3 **Shadow Usul**
2 **The Darkest Faerie**
1 **The Giant Grarrl**
1 **Koya, Korbat Huntress**
2 **Ghost Korbat**
2 **Grarrl Gladiator**

Don't play your Something Has Happened cards right away. Wait for the right time, when you can strip an important card from your opponent's hand or force him or her to draw instead of banking for the win. Experienced Neopets should be played as soon as possible, no questions asked. Finally, when you draw a Hero, wait until you can win the game or set up a win before you play them.

Hopefully, if you play well and make good use of your cards, you can use this deck to show all of your friends just what a Dark deck can do. ●

Items Galore

By: DeQuan Watson

Let's just go down the list and review the deck piece by piece. It was hard trying to decide what basic Neopets that an item heavy deck should be based on. After looking over the entire card list three or four times I decided that I wanted it to use Aishas (since one of the experienced Aishas was perfect for this) and Grarrls (so I would have some heavy hitters). Honestly and truthfully, the Aishas are more important to this deck than the Grarrls. There is the one random Green Kacheek hanging out in our deck. It is in there to help balance things out. Since it seems Air and Earth type Neopets have the higher agility, I decided to include one of them to help out in case something got a bit out of control in the agility arena.

The equipment was the easiest part of the deck to figure out. Faerie Slingshot activates whenever you use play an item. This made it an obvious perfect fit. This deck is sporting 20 items. That's half the deck. This means that the slingshot will probably end up working overtime. Snorkle was also an easy choice. This Petpet is great, because it allows you to get an additional +3 to all stats just for discarding a food card from your hand. This is another good fit, since all food cards are also items. Sceptre of Banishing is there to simply help us fight the big bad villains that get in our way. That one was a simple enough choice. Broken Sword is in the deck to help you get rid of opposing weapons obviously. It's one of the few cards you have that can do that, so use it wisely.

It was hard trying to decide what items to play. I won't go over the individual choices here, since there are so many, I will just vaguely discuss why the pile looks the way it does. Some of the items made the list simply because they have a high bank value. All of our equipment only banks for two neopoints, so if we are going to be banking items, we need them to be good. Others made the list for versatility purposes. If you have a Faerie Slingshot out, something like Everlasting Apple, becomes really insane. Other items offer a decent sized stat bonus to multiple arenas (such as Silver Negg). This is always useful in the later part of the game. The Blue Paint Brush is there to give you a boost in the agility arena and if need be, it will let you search out your Green Kacheek and get him into play.

It was fun choosing the experienced Neopets. These play a large part in the deck's strategy. The Aisha Enchantress gets an additional +2 to all stats for each item you and your opponent play in a contest. That's simply amazing in this deck. It is very likely that this Neopet will be a +4 or more to all stats every contest. The Grarrl Gladiator just makes it easier for you to win contests. Since you can win on a five or a six, your odds are increased significantly.

I feel that ALMOST every deck in Neopets needs to have a few heroes and villains. It's part of the feel of the game. But also, these cards can help you slow your opponent down when things are looking a bit grim. Shadow Usul simply made the cut because of its huge stat

line. Most importantly, it has a high agility. This is great; because it will get played in an arena that you most likely will not be fighting in. It's your weakest, so having a villain that can tie it up is great. Choosing a hero to play took a bit more thought. Jerdana ended up being chosen, because Jerdana is able to move the opposing villains around. Jerdana can get problematic villains out of the way and put them in arenas that you want them to be in. This helps a lot as a stall tactic sometimes, as you can turn your opponent's villains against them.

Well, I think that covers everything. Overall, this deck should be fairly easy to play. There aren't a lot of trick cards, so everything plays very obvious and straight forward. The most powerful cards in this deck are the equipment cards and the experienced Neopets. Don't let them go to waste. If you can get them in play and active, they should help push

the game in your favor significantly. Be aware that the agility arena is your weakest. Cards in the deck help fill that gap.

This should be a very enjoyable deck to play. It's easy and fun and it still remains competitive. ●

Neopets
3 Yellow Aisha
3 Red Aisha
3 Red Grarrl
1 Green Kacheek

Equipment
3 Faerie Slingshot
3 Snorkle
2 Sceptre of Banishing
2 Broken Sword

Items
3 Aisha Myriad
3 Everlasting Apples
3 Faerie Pancakes
3 Juppies
3 Silver Negg
3 Asparagus
2 Blue Paint Brush

Experienced Neopets
3 Aisha Enchantress
2 Grarrl Gladiator

Villains
3 Shadow Usul

Heroes
2 Jerdana

Poogle Control

By: Scott Gerhardt

I' mot going to waste much of your time getting down to the heart of this deck. This is the metamorphosis of the first deck I ever built. I came into it with the same strategy I always try to came into deck building with - take the best cards and make a deck around them.

First I started with Poogles. Their overall stats were 2-3 points higher than any other Neopet. This would give them a statistical advantage over any other deck simply based on that. I figured I could build on this, so I started with 3 each of the Yellow and Blue Poogles. Next, I needed support. One of the best experienced Neopets I could find was Grarrl Gladiator. I wanted to try to incorporate this as well, so I went with 4 Grarrls for the other basic slots. This would keep my deck to a simple theme, but incorporate things I thought would be a winning foundation for me.

Now the control part of this deck is the fact that if I am able to

gain a significant amount of card advantage and utilize cards that are reusable, then I should always be in a better position in the late game than my opponent, thus in a position to control the flow of the game at the point it needs to be controlled. This brings me to books – lots of them. This deck utilizes 14 books that yield card advantage by drawing, sifting, or returning things to your hand. This is very important, because emptying your hand can be a bad thing.

Now initial incarnations of this deck ran more books. I found this to be a problem when I could out bank my opponent 2 to 1, and still lose because all my bank cards were small. This had to change. First of all, I knew I was going to run 3

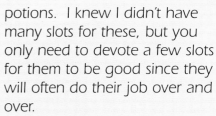

copies of Faerie Slingshot. This card is absolutely ridiculously broken and goes in most any deck. That said, natural fodders for the Slingshot were boomerang items. Of the 5, 4 of them had a bank of 3, and the Everlasting Apple has a bank of 2. Knowing that banking could be a problem, I stuck with the 4 potions. I knew I didn't have many slots for these, but you only need to devote a few slots for them to be good since they will often do their job over and over.

Still needing some bank fodder, I tracked down probably the single best "4" banker my deck could have used – Dark Faerie Token. Hopefully, this finds it's way into the bank more than not, but it can also be nice if you can to use it in a contest, especially with a Grarrl. Finally, wanting some Villain protection, I snagged 3 Jerdana's Orbs. They give decent bonuses, slaughter Villains, and bank for 3. In total, it gives me 26 bankable cards in my deck, which is very good. You never want to be stuck needing a bank card.

Moving on, we have experienced. Both Poogle Racer and Grarrl Gladiator are near the top of their class for being excellent experienced Neopets. The Gladiator doubles your odds of winning by allowing a 5 with some awesome strength, and the Racer's ability to "Shift and Swing" – moving it from one arena to another without tapping and then being able to start a contest, makes it a tremendous add. I figured this was important to see, so I stuck with the same basic ratio, and added 3 Racers and 2 Gladiators.

After playing around with a number of Heroes, I eventually settled on 2 copies of Malevolent Sentient Poogle Plushie. The plushie auto-kills all villains, and is usually a great chance at a win in the mid-to-late game, especially if a sling-shot is involved. Its ability to

run over a rival for a game-ending bank makes it invaluable.

Amongst the Something Has Happened Cards, I chose only 3 of Nothing Has Happened. I didn't feel there was a lot that added to my deck, but a number of things that could hurt it. With these 3 insurance policies in the deck, it basically assures that my deck will run the way it's supposed to without too much opponent intervention.

Finally, you must have Villains. 2 Vira and 2 Lord Darigan seemed to make the most sense. They are both good at holding down the fort while you get set up. I would have played 3 Darigan, but it's not easy to always know you'll have a Grarrl around when you need it.

The deck strategy takes some practice. Try to bank early if possible and start the card advantage. Hold off your opponent as much as possible, as some early banks could lead to trouble late. Use your books to draw and sift early. Once you're set-up with Slingshots and boomerang items, start trying to press the issue by staying in the same arenas as your opponent. Your Pets should be faster and stronger, and should win most contests, even against rivals. When it gets late, use Poogle Racer to expose open arenas and drop some of the bigger bank items for the win.

The deck will take practice, and you probably will not do well with it immediately, but it will be very good for you the more you practice with it. Good Luck! ●

Basic Neopets:

3x Blue Poogle
3x Yellow Poogle
3x Red Grarrl
1x Green Grarrl

Main Deck:
Items:

2x Dark Faerie Token
3x Jerdana's Orb
1x Essence of Brain
1x Faerie Dishwater
1x Potion of Strength
1x Potion of Speed
3x Biting Book
3x The Theives' Code
2x Beyond Neopia
3x Grimmoire of Thade
3x Hidden Tower Secrets

Equipment:

3x Faerie Slingshot

Experienced:

3x Poogle Racer
2x Grarrl Gladiator

Heroes:

2x Malevolent Sentient Poogle Plushie

Something Has Happened:

3x Nothing Has Happened

Villains

2x Lord Darigan
2x Vira

Sometimes building a deck that works can be a very difficult task, the hardest part can be making sure all the cards work well together and with only 240 cards to

Card Advantage

By: Matthew Murphy

choose from it can make for a very interesting deck. Any good deck builder will tell you that card advantage is a very key element to building a successful deck. This deck is full of card advantage; the purpose is to make sure you always have a hand full of cards by never losing your items in a contest and banking cards that replenish themselves.

The key element to this deck is Faerie Slingshot, equipment that gives a +3 bonus to all your Neopets stats when an item is playing in a contest. The best part of Faerie Slingshot is that its bonus isn't limited to one; it gives a +3 bonus for each Slingshot in play. Faerie Slingshot helps win most contests just by giving your Neopet such high stats that without rolling a 6 six most of the time your opponents Neopets stats can't match up.

Besides the Faerie Slingshot, other key elements to this deck are Potion of Strength/Speed, Faerie Dishwater, Essence of Brain, and Everlasting Apple. When these are used in a contest to give a bonus to your

Neopet's stats they will come back to your hand if you win, thus allowing you to more likely keep all the cards in your hand to reuse at a later time. They also have a bank value of 3, so when you get multiples they can be banked to help get you closer to victory. More card advantage comes from the books (Biting Book, Beyond Neopia, Hidden Tower Secrets, and The Thieves Code.) When you bank Beyond Neopia and The Thieves code they allow you to draw a card, this way you don't lose a card from your hand when you have to bank allowing for more options. When Biting Book is banked draw 2

cards and discard 2 cards. When the Hidden Tower Secrets is banked you may return up to 2 books from your discard pile to your hand, helping bring back any books that were used as stat bonus or discarded with the biting book.

When putting a deck together it is important to keep in mind the stats of your Neopets. You want to make sure that you are not too

vulnerable in any one arena, allowing your opponent to dominate the game by abusing your weakness. All around, the Eyrie's stats are average. They don't dominate in any one arena. They have a higher strength than most but are very lacking in the magic and Intelligence arenas. A great way to make up for their weakness is by playing with the experienced Neopets, Battle Eyrie and Eyrie Guard.

Battle Eyrie only has a base of 4 in the Magic arena, but add their ability to roll two dice instead of one helps give you a large advantage. Now add a Faerie Slingshot and an item, you now have a pretty good chance of winning any contest. Another Experienced Neopet that helps a lot is the Eyrie Guard. Eyrie Guard gets +3 to all stats in contests on your opponent's turn. Again when combined with a Faerie Slingshot and an item, he makes for a very large

wall when your opponent starts a contest.

The other Experienced Neopet in the deck is Fire Shoyru, When Fire Shoyru starts a contest, discard all weapons attached to its rivals. This basically makes your opponent have to move any Neopets with weapons out of the Fire Shoyru arena. A great card that works with Fire Shoyru is Secret Passages. Secret Passages allows you to move each of your untapped Neopets into an arena of your choice. This works great when your opponent is trying to dodge your Shoyru and save his weapon. This also works when trying to get that last banked card by moving one of your Neopets into an open arena.

Once this deck gets set up it is very hard for any opponent to win a contest. You will almost always have a

hand with more cards then your opponent because the return effect of the potions and the card drawing from banking your books. ●

Basic Neopets (10)

2 **Red Shoyru**
3 **Blue Shoyru**
3 **Green Eyrie**
2 **Red Eyrie**

Main Deck (41)

3 **Faerie Slingshot (equipment)**
3 **Faerie Dishawater (item)**
3 **Essence of Brain (item)**
3 **Potion of Strength (item)**
3 **Potion of Speed (item)**
2 **Everlasting Apple (item)**
3 **Biting Book (item)**
3 **Beyond Neopia (item)**
3 **Hidden Tower Secrets (item)**
3 **The Thieves Code (item)**
3 **Fire Shoyru (experienced Neopet)**
3 **Battle Eyrie (experienced Neopet)**
2 **Eyrie Guard (experienced Neopet)**
2 **Secret Passage (something has happened)**
2 **Tishi and Goliath (something has happened)**

Why Are Some People So Lucky?

By: Paul Hagan

Have you ever wondered why it seems like the same couple of people keep winning all of the tournaments? They always seem to draw all of the right cards, win all of their dice rolls, and have a firm hold on all the luck. How is that possible?

The truth is that luck has very little to do with it. The same players win because they make the right choices, not only in the game but when they are building their deck as well. What are the right choices, though?

Below are some helpful tips and hints to put you on the road to becoming a better player. Follow these suggestions, and you will be one of those people winning your local tournaments week after week.

Multiples of Cards

The best place to start is probably with your card choices. It's obvious that your deck should consist of the best cards. If one Money Tree Ghosts is good, aren't three better? One of the best ways to improve your odds of drawing the right card at the right time is to play multiples of those cards. Say you have a forty-card deck, and you really need The Giant Grarrl to help you win the game in your next turn, would you rather have a one-in-forty (2.5%) chance of drawing it or a three-in-forty chance (7.5%) of drawing it? This is one of the big reasons why

some players seem to draw the right cards all of the time: They have better odds of drawing winning cards!

Deck and Neopet Stack Size

To be brief, you should play the absolute minimum amount of cards that you possibly can. For most formats, this means a deck of exactly 40 cards and a Neopet stack of exactly 10 cards. The reasoning behind this is almost the same as the reason behind multiples of cards. Whenever you need to draw your best cards, your odds are better with a smaller deck. Say you need to draw that same The Giant Grarrl to win the game, but you only have one left in your deck. With an eighty-card deck, you have a 1-in-80 (1.25%) chance of drawing your game-winning

card, while in a forty-card deck, you have a 1-in-40 (2.5%) chance.

Playtesting

Once you have decided roughly what kind of deck you want to play, the best way to weed out the bad cards and find good cards is through playtesting. Find the best decks other people are playing, and then play against them over and over. Whenever you draw a card that

you really don't need and are upset to see, make note of it. Also make note of what cards you are always happy to see. After a load of testing, if a specific card keeps coming up as a disappointment, cut it from the deck. Likewise, if a card is great in all circumstances, play more of it. Repeat this process as much as necessary, and eventually, you will have a good, final version of your deck.

Know Your Deck

I can honestly say that almost every person I have ever seen win a tournament knew his or her deck. By this, I mean that they knew every card in it, what cards they had drawn, what cards they would draw, what cards worked well with one another, and so on. The only possible way to get in this state of mind is to play your deck over and over and over again. By the time you are ready to enter a tournament, or go play with a bunch of friends; you will be making very few mistakes and will be able to almost go on autopilot.

Always Start Contests

You should start a contest in every arena possible during your turn. Even if you have a lowly Yellow Korbat (Strength 1) and your opponent has a Red Grarrl (Strength 9), you still have a 1-in-6 (16.7%) chance of getting a 6 on your roll and winning the contest.

Retreating

Sometimes, even if you have a Neopet that only has one good attribute (Yellow Mynci with Agility 9, for example) in its home arena, it's a good thing to retreat. This could be because your opponent has gotten the upper

hand with an experienced Neopet or a Villain has just hit the board. In any case, know when to give it up and either move or trade your Neopet. Remember, free wins are always better than the giant chance of losing in a contest.

Banking and Drawing

Even though the point of the game is to reach 21 Neopoints in the bank, sometimes its better just to draw a card. Remember, every card in your hand serves a purpose besides the little coin in the bottom corner, and you should take advantage of those. Many games tend to be decided by one player using all of his or her resources early in the game to bank up to 14 or 15 points, only to be overwhelmed by an opponent who still has a hand full of cards later in the game. A good measure of the correct amount of banking and drawing is making sure you have at least two cards in your hand at all time, in case of an emergency.

Remain Calm

No matter what has happened in a game, you should always try to remain calm. Whether you start breathing deeply, become completely silent, or begin to joke with everyone around you, do whatever it takes to keep your cool. Once a

player begins to worry too much about winning or losing instead of just playing the game and having fun, they are much more likely to make a game-deciding error. Even though it's a horrible cliché, remember: winning isn't everything.

Never Give Up

The last point is often the most important, and that is definitely true in this case. The biggest piece of advice you can heed is to not give up the game until it is absolutely over. If you know that you will lose the game on your opponent's next turn, then try your best to win this turn. Although this sounds obvious, one player accepting defeat when there are still options available to him decides far too many games. If you will only win one game out of one hundred by continuing to play until the end, then that is one more game you win than you would have by quitting.

Now you know why some people are so lucky: they aren't. They just make the right choices before the game, and during it, and that leads them to more wins. By constructing your deck well, learning how to play it, and keeping the tips above in mind while playing your games, you can be one of those people. In the end, though, remember: winning isn't everything. Having fun is. ●

Working with Neggs

By: DeQuan Watson

Neggs are one of the major item types in the Neopets game. I saw some interesting interactions between them right from the get go. This made me immediately want to build a deck around them. They aren't really the most powerful type or anything, but they are definitely fun.

After looking over the spoiler list, there are a total of ten Neggs available in the first set. That's a lot to work with. I haven't run the numbers yet, but it's probably more than any other particular type of item or equipment. After playing a few games online, I noticed there are a TON of different Neggs. This is neat, because it means there are many more to come.

Let's go over the various types of Neggs.

NOTE: for the purpose of saving time we will use the following:
A = Agility,
I = Intelligence,
M = Magic,
S = Strength

FEROCIOUS NEGG - +2A, +2I

When you win a contest, search your deck for a Negg and put it into your hand.

This is one of the best Neggs. The problem is that it is extremely hard to get, since it is a foil card. I would recommend playing the full allotment of three if you are going to go Negg heavy in your deck. This is great utility; since it lets you get a Negg to help the most in any given situation.

CACKLING NEGG - +3A

You need an Earth Neopet to play this. +3A for each Negg in your bank.

This Negg is good if you plan to lock up the agility arena. A couple of these can help you win this arena easily. You can put your opponent in a position that they can only win by rolling a six. Sometimes they will still win, but now it is a one in six shot.

SILVER NEGG - +4S, +5A, +3I

Add +2 to all stats if your opponent does not play an item in this contest.

This is cool in general. This card has some strategy as to when to play

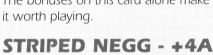

it. Try playing it during the second or third contest of the turn. Either then, or when your opponent has very few cards in hand. It's a good way to help seal the deal on a contest. I like cards with strategy and skill built into their usage and this is one of those cards. The bonuses on this card alone make it worth playing.

STRIPED NEGG - +4A

If you lose this contest, discard a Negg from your bank.

This seems like a big drawback, but it is truly worse than it is. The real reason being that this is the only Negg in the set that is worth 4NP on its own. It may or may not be a chance worth taking. If nothing else, you can simply use it as a banking only card in your deck. It still counts has a different type of Negg in your bank.

SPECKLED NEGG - +4A, +4I, +4S, +4M

If all of the cards in your bank are Neggs, this card is worth 4 neopoints. Honestly, a well balanced deck is going to have a lot of trouble having just Neggs in your bank. But, it is definitely worth it to have the chance at getting +4 to all your stats. It allows this card to be used in any arena.

There aren't many cards in the set that give bonuses greater than 2 to multiple stats, much less all four of them. I would recommend playing this even if you aren't playing a Negg heavy deck.

YELLOW NEGG - +5A, +2M, +2I

If you have at least 4 Neggs of at least 4 different names in your bank, this card is worth 4 neopoints.

I like this Negg too, but it's not as insane as some of the other. This one is simply well balanced. Also, since it is an uncommon, it's reasonably easy to get your hands on. Cards that give bonuses to multiple stats are always great.

BLUE NEGG - +3S, +4A

If you have at least 4 Neggs of at least 4 different names in

your bank, this card is worth 4 neo-points.

The multiple Negg in your bank theme is on several cards, so this just helps reinforce that concept.

BROWN NEGG - +8A

This is probably the weakest of all the Neggs. It does nothing special and has no added benefits. However, getting +8 to a stat is nothing to laugh at.

GREEN NEGG - +4A, +2M

If you have at least 4 Neggs of at least 4 different names in your bank, this card is worth 4 neopoints.

This is another one with the multiple Negg in bank requirement. It's got a nice bonus set to it, so it's definitely worth playing.

HAPPY NEGG - +2A

When you bank this card, you may take a Negg from your discard pile and put it into your hand.

At first I saw the bonus line on this Negg and thought, "Man, this must be the worst one." However, the ability is great. You don't ever truly want to have this one in play. You just want to bank it so you can recycle any lost Neggs. This helps recover Neggs that were lost in contests. Also, cards like this are greet against discard heavy decks.

Using the Neggs as part of your winning strategy can be both neat and fun. Truth be told though, at this point in the game, it's hard to get by playing ONLY Neggs as your items. With just Neggs, you will have a lot of holes to fill in your deck. You have to find some other things that work well with them.

I'd imagine after another set or two, there will be enough variability in the Neggs to allow you to play with those as your only items.

I like the interaction between these items a lot. They are reasonably simple and pretty straightforward. Another thing to remember is that these are items that are also FOOD. This is important for a few cards in the set, so you might want to search around for some interesting interactions and worth them into the same deck. One such card is Snorkle. It's a Petpet card that allows you to discard a food card to give the Neopet that it's an additional +3 to all stats. This can be huge. It can be even better if you are pretty set on winning the contest and have a Happy Negg in hand. You can then bank the Happy Negg and get back the Negg that you discarded to the Snorkle. There are a lot of small strategies like this in the game that make playing lots of cards of a particular type very interesting.

You can find several Negg decks posted on the Pojo.com message boards if you want to try and playtest one. Have fun with your Neggs.

●

Banking vs. Decking

By: DeQuan Watson

During the course of a game, there will be a ton of decisions that you will have to make. You will have to decide what Neopet to play certain items on. You will have to decide what arena to play your villains in. But, of all the decisions you will make during a game, the toughest is usually deciding whether to bank a card or draw a card after winning a contest.

On paper it seems like an extremely easy decision to have to make. You're just deciding to either get points or get a card right? Wrong. The decision is a lot more difficult than that. There are so many factors to consider.

The largest of all the factors to consider is the tightness of the game. How close is the score between you and your opponent? How close are you to winning? How close is your opponent to winning? The answers to these questions can really change your decision. If the game is close in score, you want to keep it that way. When the score is close, not only are you forced to make tough decisions, but your opponent is forced to make those same tough decisions.

Now in the unfortunate situation that your opponent has a large lead on you, you need to bank all the cards that you can.

Be very wary when your opponent reaches 15 or more points. It is very likely that they could pull a trick or two for a quick five or six points.

You'll also need to consider heavily the bank cost of your cards. Early in the game, you can afford to bank a few small point cards. But after a few turns have passed, you should be looking to bank cards of three points or more. This helps balance your game and should keep your bank total competitive.

All this time, we've been discussing the banking issues. When are the best times to draw a card? Well, to be honest, this is a much harder situation to figure out. There are a few good hints to follow though.

First and for most, check your options. If the bank costs on your cards are low, then you need to get more cards in your

hand.
Later in the game, you want to have cards that bank for three or more points. You might need to spend a few turns earlier in the game loading up your hand. Options are a good thing.

You should also think about the game state. Are you weak in a particular arena? If so, then you need to hunt down one of your villains to slow your

opponent down in that arena. Maybe your opponent has a villain that's too hard for you to deal with. If that's the case, you need to hunt down one of your heroes to help break through. The only way to do this is to draw cards.

You can always draw cards once you seal off some loose ends though. If you can lock down multiple arenas then you have more time to solidify your position. By locking up an arena, we mean that your opponent can only win by spending cards or by rolling a six on the die roll. When you can overpower an arena, good things happen. Your oppo-

nent has to spend cards to win the contest. This means that your opponent is going to have fewer cards to bank. On that same note, the threat of your opponent winning is lessened. This means that you can opt to draw more cards.

Now, it is obvious that both banking and drawing each have their own separate merits. However, this doesn't mean that that they cannot be used in conjunction with one another. You can build your deck to take advantage of both angles.

There are some cards that will allow you to draw a card when you bank a card. These types of cards take all the thought out of your decision. You can get away with banking cards and still keeping your hand size up. There are also a lot of cards that let bank a card and get another effect. Those are great. Obviously you want to get those into your bank as fast as you can. Sometimes even moving your opponent's NeoPets around can buy you turn or two.

Be sure to check out all of your cards with bonus effects. Sometimes banking cards can allow you to get cards back from your discard pile, or let you search for certain cards. Having that type of utility in your cards is great. This

can make banking a card just as good as drawing a card. These types of cards can also be a headache for your opponent. You might want to include a few of these types of cards in

your deck. There are several of them out there, so take your time and go through the set to find ones that you like.

Even though these concepts seem small, having to decide what to bank and when to draw are actually some of the largest decisions in the game. Choosing right or wrong can swing the game favorably for you or your opponent. As with everything, you will only get better with practice. Don't sweat the decisions too much though. You'll have plenty of time to get them right. ●

The Combos of Neopets

By: Scott Gerhardt

To begin this article, I'm going to tell you what a combo is. Combo, short for Combination, is a series of 2 or more cards that have an effect greater together than they might have on their own. This is one of the greatest parts about what makes any Trading card Game fun - finding and playing combos. I'm going to take this time to try to point out a number of them I have found while playing the game.

#1 – Faerie Slingshot + Earth Faerie Leaves + Everlasting Apple.

I chose Everlasting Apple for no good reason – this could be any of the 4 or so items that return to your hand if you win the contest. First of all, the Apple plus the Leaves gives you an item that you will be able to play in that contest every single time, win or lose. Knowing that you will always be able to play an item is quite an overall boost. Next, let's add in the Slingshot. The Slingshot works amazingly well with the boomerang items since it gives +3 to all

stats for whatever Neopet is in the contest regardless of the position of the Slingshot on the board. Add that to the item itself, and it gets brutal. We won't even talk about what happens when you get 2 or 3 Slingshots on the board – ugly. Adding in the Earth Faerie Leaves gives you a combo that makes you completely unafraid of your opponent rolling a 6. If they do, no big deal – the Apple comes back. A lot of Earth decks should consider this combo.

#2 – Traveling Library + Cleansing Flames + Books.

This is a combo, that if set up right, can easily win you

the game as quickly as turn 5. Light decks can easily draw a lot of cards, especially with the help of the books that allow you to draw when banked. The goal here is to utilize good bank card effects, like drawing, and not worry about their bank value. Once you are able to get about 5-6 cards in your bank, you go off. You'll need to have it set up with 2 light and 1 fire Neopet. First, tap a light to use Library. Next, do it again with the other light. You should have a ridiculous amount of cards in your hand at this point. Finally, tap the fire for Cleansing Flames, getting rid of all those cheap books and try to drop 3 and 4 point items. With 6 items, it's pretty easy to hit 21 and win on the spot.

#3 – Kacheek Thief + Secret Passage

This is a very control-based combo, being used to insure your opponent's bank total remains low. Since this combo leads towards a deck that has you banking less, make sure your banks will count. In this game, you will only be able to stop your opponent from banking so many times. They will get some cards into the bank. They also can only hold down 3 arenas at a time. Using this combo, you can very quickly set up your Kacheek Thief into the empty arena(s), and use their abilities to keep your opponent's bank empty.

Play an Equipment heavy deck and you can blitz through it pretty fast with some rather beefy Neopets along the way.

#5 – Jeran's Armour + Peachpa

The Armour is an obvious combo with Jeran's Sword, but is not as obviously a combo with Peachpa. Peachpa is a nice little fruit that gives a couple of very nice bonuses for an item, but doesn't work if your opponent plays an item.

#4 – Rainbow Swirly Thing + Battle Eyrie

The Swirly Thing and many other cards are pretty bad. They are bad because they require a 6 to have almost any effect. So why not increase the chances of them working by adding in the Eyrie, which lets you roll 2 dice, doubling your chances at the auto-win. While the chances of 1 in 6 are bad, they're not nearly as bad when they are 1 in.

Luckily, Jeran's Armour keeps them from playing an item, allowing good 'ole Peachpa to do its worst without fear of being discarded. This would sure help make a fruit/food deck run a lot easier. ●

Top 5 Basic Neopets

Many of the basic Neopets do a lot of the same things. This made selecting a top 5 here extremely difficult. But at the moment, with the current state of the game, here are the basics that made my top five list. These five Neopets just barely edged out the rest of them.

By: DeQuan Watson

Blue Poogle

The stat line on this basic Neopet is amazing. It has a 6/4/5/6 line. That's great. However, this Neopet is so amazing because you get a +1 to all stats in contests on your turn. That's insane. It's very hard to keep from saying, "Put three of these in everyone one of your Neopets decks." The card is simply that good. Think about it. On your turn it is effectively a 7/5/6/7. That's by far the best you are going to pull together on a basic Neopet. After evaluating it, take a look at how awesome it gets with some added equipment.

Red Shoyru

The Red Shoyru is on this list for nothing else but game balance. This is a Neopet that you are never upset to draw. It gives you a fighting chance in every arena. It's good to know that you'll never have less than a four in any arena. Granted, a four isn't super, but it's far from bad. This Neopet can help you balance a deck and minimize your witnesses.

Red Korbat

This guy isn't exceptionally amazing, but does still seem to be quite popular. Since so many people like playing with Dark neopets, you can expect to see a lot of these around. What makes this little gem so surprising is that it comes in every starter deck. I'm sure both of these factors are what keep Red Korbat popping up in a lot of decks.

Red Lupe

I'm personally a fan of the villains that require Earth Neopets, so that's one of the reasons that this guy made the list. More importantly, with a 6/2/5/5 stat line, it gives you a nice balance to play with. You don't want to have Neopets that are linear. You want to have a decent shot in every arena and this guy helps. Red Lupe also gets a +2 to all stats against Air rivals. This helps against those bothersome Eyries.

Green Kacheek

The Green Kacheek is a Light type Neopet. This is good, because several of the Something Has Happened cards require you to have a light Neopet. But even with that fact aside, it comes with a decent stat line. That's not all though. It also gets a bonus from against Dark Neopets. You get a +2 against all Dark Neopets. As it stands, dark is probably the most played type of Neopet in the game. This gives you an edge in quite a few matchups.

Top 5 Villains

By: DeQuan Watson

Villains might be some of the most under rated card types in the game. They don't do much on their own merits. However, they take up space in arenas you don't feel like fighting in and slow your opponent down. Sometimes that's all you need.

Lord Darigan

Lord Darigan is a very interesting card. It's a Villain that actually helps your Neopets. All Dark Neopets get +1 to all stats while Lord Darigan is in play. Also, Lord Darigan only has one stat that is below 15. This makes him a very formidable opponent is every way. Every deck that's heavy on Dark Neopets definitely needs to play three of these. Not only does it hinder your opponent's progress, it helps you win more contests. You can't ask for much more than that out of any card.

Evil Sloth Clone #238

This Villain only has two strong stats (strength and agility). That is not a big deal really. The trick to this guy is that he lets you keep perpetual Villains in play. When this Villain comes into play you get to search your deck for another Evil Sloth Clone #238. This can allow you to have a Villain on the table for several turns. If you're trying to tie up a game to buy yourself some time and slowly put it out of reach, this could be your man for the job.

Werelupe Sage

Everyone knows that you want some versatility with your Neopets and Heroes. What people don't think about is that versatility in your Villains can be equally as good. The Werelupe Sage has high stats in everything but Agility. This means that you can use it multiple arenas. He's also good in a pinch to just buy you a turn if you need it late in the game. This isn't a Villain that is going to totally swing games, but it's a good solid Villain for decks heavy on Earth Neopets can play.

MAGAX: Destroyer

This guy is on the list just because of maneuverability. This is very neat. This guy requires you to have a Fire Neopet to come into play. But that just means that you are already set to use his ability, if you can put a Fire Neopet into his arena to move him to a different arena. This doesn't seem like that big of a deal, but if your opponent has gotten away from your villain or found a way around it, you can put MAGAX back where you need him.

Jhudora

Jhudora has two stats that are above 20. This is going to make it hard for your opponent to get rolling in the Magic and Intelligence arenas. Jhudora's ability doesn't allow anyone to bank cards without first discarding a card. However, if you are playing a deck that is made to control your opponents hand size, then this Villain is perfect for your deck. She doesn't fit in any many decks, but the ones she does, she can be devastating.

Heroes can play a big part in a game. The odds are you won't be packing very many of them in your deck. But you want them handy for those arenas that become hard to break through.

Top 5 Heroes

By: DeQuan Watson

Malevolent Sentient Poogle Plushie

This Hero is very misleading because of it's stat line (1/1/1/1). Technically, this Hero doesn't need to have high stats at all. It makes all of it's rivals stats a zero. They will still get bonuses from outside items. This Neopet works for both Dark and Water decks, so it's got some serious potential. That's a lot of power from a crazy plushie.

Jerdana

Jerdana's uses are limited, but they extremely powerful when they come into play. If your opponent's are using lots of villains that are making your life miserable, you can call on Jerdana to help. When you play Jerdana, you can move a villain of your choice to the same arena as long as there isn't one there currently. This isn't an ability that's useful all the time, but it's extremely helpful.

Jeran

Jeran is a very interesting Hero. His versatility is what makes him amazing. He has three stats that are over 10 and one of those is a 21 strength. You can tap an Earth or a Light Neopet to get it into play. This allows it to be played in more decks. Another cool thing about Jeran is that he can manipulate your opponent's Dark Neopets by bringing them into his arena. This can effectively buy you a turn or two.

Torshac, Shoyru Scout

The is one of the most manipulative cards in the game. Torshac is an awesome hero to have in play. The turn that you have this Hero in play, you can play items in your contests after the die roll instead of before. This is great. You don't waste items needlessly, especially if you were to roll a six. This means you get more cards to bank. Even if it is for just one turn, you can use this Hero to get you a jump on the competition.

Grey Faerie

For a hero, the Grey Faerie's stats aren't all that impressive. But this card allows from some great deck building strategies. You can play different types of Neopets in the same deck with the help of the Grey Faerie. You can tap any Neopet to put the Grey Faerie into play. Also, while the Grey Faerie is in play, you can play cards in your hand with ANY type of Neopet you have in play, even if the type isn't the one normally required. This helps a lot in making sure that your hand isn't clogged up with unplayable cards. The strategies that this card opens up are endless.

Top 5 Experienced Neopets

At a quick glance, all of the experienced Neopets seem useful and devastating. Many seem almost broken or game breaking. This was a fun list to put together.

By: DeQuan Watson

Battle Eyrie

When I was first learning the game, this was one of my favorite experienced Neopets. The stat line is pretty weak for an experienced Neopet (8/7/4/3). This seems pretty mediocre. That's not what makes this Neopet so good. This Neopets special ability is that you get to roll an additional die during contests. This is amazingly helpful. It makes winning contests a little easier. More importantly, it gives you double the chances of rolling a six for an auto-win.

Fire Shoyru

This guy boasts a pretty powerful 7/11/6/7 stat line. >From an agility standpoint, this guy is a house. But you can ignore that altogether if you like. The special ability that this Neopet has is devastating. When you start a contest with this Neopet, you get to destroy not one, but all weapons attached to a rival Neopet. That can make winning some contests extremely easy. Once this guy hits the table, your opponents plays can become extremely limited.

Grarrl Gladiator

This experienced Neopet brings an amazing 14 strength stat to the table. This is as good as many of the villains and heroes. This means that this guy can plow through nearly anything in strength contests. The kicker to this guy is that you can win contests on a five or a six. This now gives you a one in three shot of winning any contest regardless of the situation. That's definitely nothing to laugh at.

Korbat Researcher

This experienced Neopet is great. The only downside is that you have to build a deck to take advantage of it. Korbat Researcher does offer a 13 intelligence (must be all that reading). This Neopet is one of the ones you want when you are trying to cycle through your deck looking for a particular card. When you bank a book, you get to draw a card and then discard one. It doesn't help get you more cards, it just helps you hunt down the card you want.

Mynci Inventor

Many people will look at this and think that I'm crazy, but this card is great. The stats on it are really low for an experienced Neopet. However, it allows you to break part of the game. You get to bankcards every turn while drawing cards. When you bank an equipment card with this Neopet you get to draw a card. This gives you cards for banking and keeps card advantage. You have to build a deck to take advantage of it, but it's well worth it.

Top 5 Items

Items are the heart and soul of contests. You need to have these to help win contests in order to bank cards. Without these, your deck almost can't function.

By: DeQuan Watson

Jerdana's Orb

This card can almost be called 'The Villain Killer.' This is amazing. It gives one of your neopets +10 to all stats against Villains. This means that it obviously only works against villains and is a dead card in your hand the rest of the time. This is a bit unfortunate. However, if you only have one or two in your deck, they shouldn't get in the way. Also, your odds of taking out a Villain go way up when you have +10 to a stat. This item also banks for three neopoints, so it you get stuck with it, it's not completely dead weight.

Kauvara's Potion

This is a very tricky card to use. I'd recommend staying away from it if you don't know your deck real well. However, this item can be used on its own in the Magic arena. After all, a +6 bonus is never bad. But it's ability is just as good, if not better. You can discard this card before you roll to get an item from your discard pile and use it in the current contest. If you had something get wasted earlier, you can take advantage of it. It's even better if the new item returns to your hand.

Hubrid's Puzzle Box

We all like playing cards that give us big bonuses. The bonuses offered by this card are easily up there with the best of them. This card gives +1 to all stats for each card in your opponent's bank. After the first four turns of the game, this card is pretty amazing. Since it gives a bonus to all stats, you can use it in every arena. This card is strong in every way.

Potion of Sludge

This card banks for three neopoints. That's not bad. This card gives you a +5 bonus in the Magic arena. That's not bad. Wait a minute. It says here if you win a contest by rolling a six, you can remove a card from your opponent's bank. Removing cards from your opponent's bank is pretty good I'd imagine. This card can sit at number two.

Aisha Myriad

What's better than getting the bonus of an item? That's easy...getting the bonus of multiple items in a turn. When you play this card, you reveal the top four cards and get to use all of the items that are in those top four cards. Getting the bonuses would be good enough. It doesn't stop there though. You also get all of the contest effects of those cards. To add insult to injury, it banks for three points. There's not a single things bad about this card.

Top 5 Equipment

Equipment cards can make some really weak Neopets really strong. They do a variety of things in addition to giving statistical bonuses. Here are some of the best ones out there.

By: DeQuan Watson

Doglefox

Doglefox is both aggressive and defensive at the same time. It gives a bonus to every stat. That's already good in and of itself. That's not all it does though. It also negates all the bonuses that your opponent's Petpets give. That's right, it makes rival petpets 0 stats. This can make many cards in your opponent's deck useless. He's also quite cute.

Broken Sword

The bonuses from this card aren't all that special. The fact that it destroys equipment is. Its a very good, efficient, and effective way to get rid of equipment on your opponent's Neopets. It's a common, so it's easy to get your hands on. That fact has kept this card at least slightly popular. This card is definitely not the most powerful on this list, but we can all agree that's it very handy to have around.

Earth Faerie Leaves

How many times have you gotten discouraged because you've played an item that went to waste, because you lost the roll? Well, with this equipment, that becomes much less of an issue. If you play an item in a contest involving the equipped Neopet and you lose, you simply get to put the item back in your hand. This is great. You can take a chance on winning and if things don't go your way, use it for your next contest. This can drive your opponent crazy. It also can let you stay ahead on the card count when it comes to banking cards.

Night Stone

Night Stone is very devastating. This card keeps your opponent from rolling dice in contests against a Neopet equipped with this item. That's a huge change in the game for your side. It ensures that your opponent will have to play items or equipment to win any contests involving the equipped Neopet. This leaves them fewer cards to bank. To top it off, it means you don't have to worry about the auto-wins on the six. This is almost a must have equipment card.

Faerie Slingshot

This card is by all accounts, simply ridiculous. It offers a small stat bonus of its own, but it's the special ability of this weapon that makes it so good. When you play an item in a contest in ANY arena, the Faerie Slingshot adds +3 to all stats. That's just crazy! This is easily at the top of the list. Bonus damage in every arena never hurts. You can even use any type of Neopet to play the card. This means that it fits in nearly any deck.

Top 5 Something Has Happened

By: DeQuan Watson

These cards can be played at different times throughout the game for some devastating effects. Most decks won't have a lot of these, but the ones that get played are going to be good.

Darigan's Blight

Sometimes you just really need to slow your opponent down. What's the best way to do that? Well, to play a Villain of course. What happens if there's not a Villain in your hand? Well, that's what Darigan's Blight is for. It lets you search your deck for one a Villain and add it to your hand. This card is especially great if you only play three copies of one Villain. Being able to get the Villain you want when you want them is a very good thing.

Sloth's Master Plan

When you look at various cards to put in your deck, you are always looking for offensive cards. This card is more of a defensive card. When your opponent makes the playing field too difficult for you to win contests with the help of his Villains, this card is what you need. It allows you to remove ALL Villains in play. In addition to having an Earth Neopet in play, you need to discard another card to play Sloth's Master Plan. It's a price that's definitely worth playing though.

Morphing Runes

This card is a very fun, sneaky card. You can lull your opponent into a false sense of security and then surprise them. Because you get to use the stats of your choice, you get a lot of flexibility. You can make your opponent waste cards needlessly. You can move your Neopets around and still have the advantage. You can run from Villains and still get to win a contest or two in an arena that you would normally be weak in.

Traveling Library

This card is simply amazing. You get to draw a card for each book that you've banked. This is huge, since a lot of the useful books have a very low bank value. This is one of the key cards to book based decks. Card advantage can be huge late in the game after you and your opponent have played out many items from your hands. This helps you stock back up and find those higher neopoint cards to finish the game.

Nothing Has Happened

What can be better than all the other Something Has Happened cards? Well, the one that stops them all of course. All you need is a Water Neopet on your side ready to go. This card can go a long way to put a halt to your opponent's tricks. With this in your hand, you have no fear of your opponent surprising you with a Something Has Happened card at all. This card is easily one of the strongest card in the game. Just be aware that if your opponent has a Water Neopet out, this card could be waiting for you.

Top 10 Overall
By: DeQuan Watson

Well, I guess I need to go through the entire card set and make a solid top 10. Scott Gerhardt reviewed each and an every card earlier in the book. I have not seen his reviews, and my reviews are totally independent of his. Look at his 4 star and 5 star cards to get a feel for Scott's Top Cards. Here are my choices for the current top 10 cards in the neopets card game.

Korbat Researcher
Getting to looks at extra cards is good. This is the king of card advantage among experienced neopets.

Mynci Inventor
You get to bank a card AND draw a card. There's not much better than that. It's the classic two for one.

Traveling Library
Getting to draw up extra cards late in the game is a very good thing. Winning gets a lot easier when you have a fistful of options.

Faerie Slingshot
This card gives an added bonus from any-where on the field, as long as you play an item. It's a bonus on top of a bonus.

Night Stone
This crazy card puts your rival neopets into a bit of a bind. This makes them really scramble to find a way to win in the prob-lem arena.

Lord Darigan
This guy is simply amazing. Not only can you cause problems for your opponent, you can enhance your own neopets to aid in your victory run.

Aisha Myriad
You have the potential of getting to use the bonus of up to five total items in one con-test. Those are numbers you want to have in your favor.

Nothing Has Happened
This seems a bit high on our list, but any card than can just outright stop a bunch of other cards has to be good.

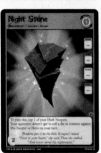

Grey Faerie
This card probably allows more deck creativ-ity than any other card in the game. Having the right type of neopet in play is no longer an issue.

Blue Poogle
This may not be the strongest card in the game on it's own. However, if you want to fill a slot in your neopets deck, this guy is ALWAYS a candidate.